KING
WARRIOR
MAGICIAN
LOVER

KING
WARRIOR
MAGICIAN
LOVER

Rediscovering the Archetypes of the Mature Masculine

Robert Moore and Douglas Gillette

HarperSanFrancisco
A Division of HarperCollinsPublishers

Audio tapes of Robert Moore's lectures, which form the foundation for much of the material in this book, may be purchased by writing to the C. G. Jung Institute of Chicago, 550 Callan Avenue, Evanston, IL 60202.

FIRST EDITION

Library of Congress Cataloging-in-Publication Data
Moore, Robert L.
    King, warrior, magician, lover : rediscovering the archetypes of
the mature masculine / Robert Moore and Douglas Gillette.—1st ed.
    p. cm.
    Includes bibliographical references.
    ISBN 0–06–250597–1
    1. Men—Psychology. 2. Masculinity (Psychology). I. Gillette,
Douglas. II. Title.
HQ1090.M66 1990
155.6'32—dc20   89–45991
                                                                CIP

90 91 92 93 94 RRD(H) 10 9 8 7 6 5 4 3 2 1

This edition is printed on acid-free paper that meets the American National Standards Institute Z39.48 Standard.

To the poet Robert Bly, who has provided the impetus
for a revaluing of the masculine experience.

Four Mighty Ones are in every Man; a Perfect Unity
Cannot Exist but from the Universal Brotherhood of Eden,
The Universal Man, to Whom be Glory Evermore. Amen.
—William Blake, *The Four Zoas*

Contents

Preface

The archetypes of King, Warrior, Magician, and Lover have been increasingly in focus in men's gatherings and publications in the United States and abroad. Indeed, many people assume that these patterns have traditionally been understood to be the building blocks of the mature masculine. In fact, the psychological research that led to the naming of these archetypes as the four fundamental configurations which, in dynamic relationship, constitute the deep structures of the mature male psyche was first presented in a series of lectures at the C. G. Jung Institute of Chicago and first published in a series of best-selling audiotapes now widely influential in the men's movement. It is our belief that the psychological findings outlined in these lectures constitute a major and potentially revolutionary breakthrough in decoding the fundamental deep structures of the human self, both masculine and feminine. This decoding of what Carl Jung called the "double quaternio" builds on Jung's understanding of the archetypal Self, but extends our grasp of inner geography beyond Jung's work by clearly delineating not only the psychological contents and potentials imaged in the "four quarters," but also the two fundamental dialectical oppositions built into the dynamics of the deep self: King (or Queen)/Magician and Lover/Warrior.

King, Warrior, Magician, Lover is an exploratory survey of the implications of this research for understanding the masculine psyche. It is the first of a forthcoming five-volume series on masculine psychology based on this paradigm. Subsequent volumes are planned that will elaborate the wider implicatons of this theoretical model for human psychology and spirituality. Those with technical professional interests or who find their curiosity stimulated and want to know more should consult the list of resources provided at the back of the book.

Our purpose in writing this book, however, has been to offer men a simplified and readable outline of an "operator's manual for the male psyche." Reading this book should help you understand your strengths and weaknesses as a man and provide you with a map to the territories of masculine selfhood which you still need to explore.

Acknowledgments

The authors wish to thank Robert Bly for his encouragement, Graciela Infante for her careful reading of the manuscript, Margaret Shanahan and Graciela Infante for their many helpful suggestions, Patrick Nugent for his absolutely accurate transcription of Robert Moore's lecture tapes, and the editorial and production staff of HarperSanFrancisco. In addition, we wish to offer special appreciation to the many men who have reflected on their personal experience in terms of this new approach to masculine psychology and have helped us to refine and deepen our understanding.

Introduction

During Bill Moyers's recent interview with the poet Robert Bly, "A Gathering of Men," a young man asked the question, "Where are the initiated men of power today?" We have written this book in order to answer this question, which is on the minds of both men and women. In the late twentieth century, we face a crisis in masculine identity of vast proportions. Increasingly, observers of the contemporary scene— sociologists, anthropologists, and depth psychologists—are discovering the devastating dimensions of this phenomenon, which affects each of us personally as much as it affects our society as a whole. Why is there so much gender confusion today, at least in the United States and Western Europe? It seems increasingly difficult to point to anything like either a masculine or a feminine essence.

We can look at family systems and see the breakdown of the traditional family. More and more families display the sorry fact of the disappearing father, which disappearance, through either emotional or physical abandonment, or both, wreaks psychological devastation on the children of both sexes. The weak or absent father cripples both his daughters' and his sons' ability to achieve their own gender identity and to relate in an intimate and positive way with members both of their own sex and the opposite sex.

But it is our belief and experience that we can't just point in any simple way to the disintegration of modern family systems, important as this is, to explain the crisis in masculinity. We have to look at two other factors that underlie this very disintegration.

First, we need to take very seriously the disappearance of *ritual processes* for initiating boys into manhood. In traditional societies there are standard definitions of what makes up what we call Boy psychology and Man psychology. This can be seen clearly in the tribal societies that have come under the careful scrutiny of such noted anthropologists as Arnold van Gennep and Victor Turner. There are carefully constructed rituals for helping the boys of the tribe make the transition to manhood. Over the centuries of civilization in the West, almost all these ritual processes have been abandoned or have been diverted into narrower and less energized channels—into phenomena we can call *pseudo-initiations.*

We can point to the historical background for the decline of ritual initiation. The Protestant Reformation and the Enlightenment were strong movements that shared the theme of the discrediting of ritual process. And once ritual as a sacred and transforming process has been discredited, what we are left with is what Victor Turner has called "mere ceremonial," which does not have the power necessary to achieve genuine transformation of consciousness. By disconnecting from ritual we have done away with the processes by which both men and women achieved their gender identity in a deep, mature, and life-enhancing way.

What happens to a society if the ritual processes by which these identities are formed become discredited? In the case of men, there are many who either had no initiation into manhood or who had pseudo-initiations that failed to evoke the needed transition into adulthood. We get the dominance of Boy psychology. Boy psychology is everywhere around us, and its marks are easy to see. Among them are abusive and violent acting-out behaviors against others, both men and women; passivity and weakness, the inability to act effectively and creatively in one's own life and to engender life and creativity in others (both men and women); and, often, an oscillation between the two—abuse/weakness, abuse/weakness.

Along with the breakdown of meaningful ritual process for masculine initiation, a second factor seems to be contributing to the dissolution of mature masculine identity. This factor, shown to us by one strain of feminist critique, is called patriarchy. Patriarchy is the social and cultural organization that has ruled our Western world, and much of the rest of the globe, from at least the second millennium B.C.E. to the present. Feminists have seen how male dominance in patriarchy has been oppressive and abusive of the feminine—of both the so-called feminine characteristics and virtues and actual women themselves. In their radical critique of patriarchy, some feminists conclude that masculinity in its roots is essentially abusive, and that connection with "eros"—with love, relatedness, and gentleness—comes only from the feminine side of the human equation.

As useful as some of these insights have been to the cause of both feminine and masculine liberation from patriarchal stereotypes, we believe there are serious problems with this perspective. In our view, patriarchy is *not* the expression of deep and rooted masculinity, for truly deep and rooted masculinity is *not* abusive. Patriarchy is the expression of the *immature* masculine. It is the expression of Boy psychology, and, in part, the shadow—or crazy—side of masculinity. It expresses the stunted masculine, fixated at immature levels.

Patriarchy, in our view, is an attack on *masculinity* in its fullness as well as femininity in its fullness. Those caught up in the structures and dynamics of patriarchy seek to dominate not only women but men as well. Patriarchy is based on fear—the boy's fear, the immature masculine's fear—of women, to be sure, but also fear of men. Boys fear women. They also fear real men.

The patriarchal male does not welcome the full masculine development of his sons or his male subordinates any more than he welcomes the full development of his daughters, or his female employees. This is the story of the superior at the office who can't stand it that we are as good as we are. How often we are envied, hated, and attacked in direct and passive-aggressive ways even as we seek to unfold who we really are in all our beauty, maturity, creativity, and generativity! The more beautiful, competent, and creative we become, the more we seem to invite the hostility of our superiors, or even of our peers. What we are really being attacked by is the immaturity in human beings who are terrified of our advances on the road toward masculine or feminine fullness of being.

Patriarchy expresses what we are calling Boy psychology. It is not an expression of mature masculine potentials in their essence, in the fullness of their being. We have come to this conclusion from our study of ancient myths and modern dreams, from our examination from the inside of the rapid feminization of the mainline religious community, from our reflection upon the rapid changes in gender roles in our society as a whole, and from our years of clinical practice, in which we have become increasingly aware that something vital is missing in the inner lives of many of the men who seek psychotherapy.

What is missing is not, for the most part, what many depth psychologists assume is missing; that is, adequate connection with the inner *feminine*. In many cases, these men seeking help had been, and were continuing to be, *overwhelmed* by the feminine. What they were missing was an adequate connection to the deep and instinctual *masculine* energies, the potentials of mature masculinity. They were being blocked from connection to these potentials by patriarchy itself, and by the feminist critique upon what little masculinity they could still hold onto for themselves. And they were being blocked by the lack in their lives of any meaningful and transformative initiatory process by which they could have achieved a sense of manhood.

We found, as these men sought their own experience of masculine structures through meditation, prayer, and what Jungians call active imagination, that as they got more and more in touch with the inner archetypes of mature masculinity, they were increasingly able to let go of their patriarchal self- and other-wounding thought, feeling, and behavior patterns and become more genuinely strong, centered, and generative toward themselves and others—*both* women and men.

In the present crisis in masculinity we do not need, as some feminists are saying, *less* masculine power. We need *more*. But we need more of the *mature* masculine. We need more Man psychology. We need to develop a sense of calmness about masculine power so we don't have to act out dominating, disempowering behavior toward others.

There is too much slandering and wounding of both the masculine and the feminine in patriarchy, as well as in the feminist reaction against patriarchy. The feminist critique, when it is not wise enough, actually further wounds an already besieged authentic masculinity. It may be that, in truth, there never has been a time yet in human history when mature masculinity (or mature femininity) was really in ascendancy. We can't be sure of that. What we can be sure of is that mature masculinity is not in the ascendant today.

We need to learn to love and be loved by the mature masculine. We need to learn to celebrate authentic masculine power and potency, not only for the sake of our personal well-being as men and for our relationships with others, but also because the crisis in mature masculinity feeds into the global crisis of survival we face as a species. Our dangerous and unstable world urgently needs mature men and mature women if our race is going to go on at all into the future.

Because there is little or no ritual process in our society capable of boosting us from Boy psychology into Man psychology, we each must go on our own (with each other's help and support) to the deep sources of masculine energy potentials that lie within us all. We must find a way of connecting with these sources of empowerment. This book, we hope, will contribute to our successful accomplishment of this vital task.

PART I

*From Boy Psychology
to Man Psychology*

1. *The Crisis in Masculine Ritual Process*

We hear it said of some man that "he just can't get himself together." What this means, on a deep level, is that so-and-so is not experiencing, and cannot experience, his deep cohesive structures. He is fragmented; various parts of his personality are split off from each other and leading fairly independent and often chaotic lives. A man who "cannot get it together" is a man who has probably not had the opportunity to undergo ritual initiation into the deep structures of manhood. He remains a boy—not because he wants to, but because no one has shown him the way to transform his boy energies into man energies. No one has led him into direct and healing experiences of the inner world of the masculine potentials.

When we visit the caves of our distant Cro-Magnon ancestors in France, and descend into the dark of those otherworldly, and inner-worldly, sanctuaries and light our lamps, we jump back in startled awe and wonder at the mysterious, hidden wellsprings of masculine might we see depicted there. We feel something deep move within us. Here, in silent song, the magic animals—bison, antelope, and mammoth—leap and thunder in pristine beauty and force across the high, vaulted ceilings and the undulating walls, moving purposefully into the shadows of the folds of the rock, then springing at us again in the light of our lamps. And here, painted with them, are the handprints of men, of the artist-hunters, the ancient warriors and providers, who met here and performed their primeval rituals.

Anthropologists are almost universally agreed that these cave sanctuaries were created, in part at least, by men for men and specifically for the ritual initiation of boys into the mysterious world of male responsibility and masculine spirituality.

But ritual process for the making of men out of boys is not limited to our conjectures about these ancient caves. As many scholars have shown, most notable among them Mircea Eliade and Victor Turner, ritual initiatory process still survives in tribal cultures to this day, in Africa, South America, islands in the South Pacific, and many other places. It survived until very recent times among the Plains Indians of North America. The study of ritual process by the specialist may tend toward dry reading. But we may see it enacted colorfully in a number of contemporary movies. Movies are like ancient folktales and myths. They are stories we tell ourselves about ourselves—about our lives and their meaning. In fact, initiatory process for both men and women is one of the great hidden themes of many of our movies.

A good, explicit example of this can be found in the movie *The Emerald Forest*. Here, a white boy has been captured and raised by Brazilian Indians. One day, he's playing in the river with a beautiful girl. The chief has noticed his interest in the girl for some time. This awakening of sexual interest in the boy is a signal to the wise chief. He appears on the riverbank with his wife and some of the tribal elders and surprises Tomme (Tommy) at play with the girl. The chief booms out, "Tomme, your time has come to die!" Everyone seems profoundly shaken. The chief's wife, playing the part of all women, of all mothers, asks, "Must he die?" The chief threateningly replies, "Yes!" Then, we see a firelit nighttime scene in which Tomme is seemingly tortured by the older men in the tribe; and forced into the forest vines, he is being eaten alive by jungle ants. He writhes in agony, his body mutilated in the jaws of the hungry ants. We fear the worst.

Finally, the sun comes up, though, and Tomme, still breathing, is taken down to the river by the men and bathed, the clinging ants washed from his body. The chief then raises his voice and says, "The boy is dead and the man is born!" And with that, he is given his first spiritual experience, induced by a drug blown through a long pipe into his nose. He hallucinates and in his hallucination discovers his animal soul (an eagle) and soars above the world in new and expanded consciousness, seeing, as if from a God's-eye view, the totality of his jungle world. Then he is allowed to marry. Tomme is a man. And, as he takes on a man's responsibilities and identity, he is moved first into the position of a brave in the tribe and then into the position of chief.

It can be said that life's perhaps most fundamental dynamic is the attempt to move from a lower form of experience and consciousness to a higher (or deeper) level of consciousness, from a diffuse identity to a more consolidated and structured identity. All of human life at least attempts to move forward along these lines. We seek initiation into adulthood, into adult responsibilities and duties toward ourselves and others, into adult joys and adult rights, and into adult spirituality. Tribal societies had highly specific notions about adulthood, both masculine and feminine, and how to get to it. And they had ritual processes like the one in *The Emerald Forest* to enable their children to achieve what we could call calm, secure maturity.

Our own culture has pseudo-rituals instead. There are many pseudo-initiations for men in our culture. Conscription into the military is one. The fantasy is that the humiliation and forced nonidentity of boot camp will "make a man out of you." The gangs of our major cities are another manifestation of pseudo-initiation and so are the prison systems, which, in large measure, are run by gangs.

We call these phenomena pseudo-events for two reasons. For one thing, with the possible exception of military initiation, these processes, though sometimes highly ritualized (especially within city gangs), more often than not initiate the boy into a kind of masculinity that is skewed, stunted, and false. It is a patriarchal "manhood," one that is abusive of others, and often of self. Sometimes a ritual murder is required of the would-be initiate. Usually the abuse of drugs is involved in the gang culture. The boy may become an acting-out adolescent in these systems and achieve a level of development roughly parallel to the level expressed by the society as a whole in its boyish values, though in a contra-cultural form. But these pseudo-initiations will not produce men, because real men are not wantonly violent or hostile. Boy psychology, which we'll look at in more detail in chapter 3, is charged with the struggle for dominance of others, in some form or another. And it is often caught up in the wounding of self, as well as others. It is sadomasochistic. Man psychology is always the opposite. It is nurturing and generative, not wounding and destructive.

In order for Man psychology to come into being for any particular man, there needs to be a death. Death—symbolic, psychological, or spiritual—is always a vital part of any initiatory ritual. In psychological terms, the boy Ego must "die." The old ways of being and doing and thinking and feeling must ritually "die," before the new man can emerge. Pseudo-initiation, though placing some curbs on the boy Ego, often amplifies the Ego's striving for power and control in a new form, an adolescent form regulated by other adolescents. Effective, transformative initiation absolutely slays the Ego and its desires in its old form to resurrect it with a new, subordinate relationship to a previously unknown power or center. Submission to the power of the mature masculine energies always brings forth a new masculine personality that is marked by calm, compassion, clarity of vision, and generativity.

A second factor makes most initiations in our culture pseudo-initiations. In most cases, there simply is not a contained ritual process. Ritual process is contained by two things. The first is sacred space and the second is a ritual elder, a "wise old man" or a "wise old woman" who is completely trustworthy for the initiate and can lead the initiate through the process and deliver him (or her) intact and enhanced on the other side.

Mircea Eliade researched the role of sacred space extensively. He concluded that space that has been ritually hallowed is essential to initiations of every kind. In tribal societies this space can be a specially constructed hut or house in which the boys awaiting their initiation are held. It can be a cave. Or it can be the vast wilderness into which the would-be initiate is driven in order to die or to find his manhood. The sacred space can be the "magic circle" of magicians. Or, as in more advanced civilizations, it can be an inner room in the precincts of a great temple. This space must be sealed from the influence of the outside world, especially, in the case of boys, from the influence of women. Often, the initiates are put through terrifying emotional and excruciatingly painful physical trials. They learn to submit to the pain of life, to the ritual elders, and to the masculine traditions and myths of the society. They are taught all the secret wisdom of men. And they are released from the sacred space only when they have successfully completed the ordeal and been reborn as men.

The second essential ingredient for a successful initiatory process is the presence of a ritual elder. In *The Emerald Forest* this is the chief and the other elders of the tribe. The ritual elder is the man who knows the secret wisdom, who knows the ways of the tribe and the closely guarded men's myths. He is the one who lives out of a vision of mature masculinity.

With a scarcity in our culture of mature men, it goes without saying that ritual elders are in desperately short supply. Thus, pseudo-initiations remain skewed toward the reinforcement of Boy psychology rather than allowing for movement toward Man psychology, even if some sort of ritual process exists, and even if a kind of sacred space has been set up on the city streets or on the cell block.

The crisis in mature masculinity is very much upon us. Lacking adequate models of mature men, and lacking the societal cohesion and institutional structures for actualizing ritual process, it's "every man for himself." And most of us fall by the wayside, with no idea what it was that was the goal of our gender-drive or what went wrong in our strivings. We just know we are anxious, on the verge of feeling impotent, helpless, frustrated, put down, unloved and unappreciated, often ashamed of being masculine. We just know that our creativity was attacked, that our initiative was met with hostility, that we were ignored, belittled, and left holding the empty bag of our lost self-esteem. We cave in to a dog-eat-dog world, trying to keep our work and our relationships afloat, losing energy, or missing the mark. Many of us seek the generative, affirming, and empowering father (though most of us don't know it), the father who, for most of us, never existed in our actual lives and won't appear, no matter how hard we try to make him appear.

However, as students of human mythology, and as Jungians, we believe there is good news. It's this good news for men (as well as women) that we want to share. And it is to this that we now turn.

2. *Masculine Potentials*

Those of us who have been influenced by the thinking of the great Swiss psychologist Carl Jung have great reason to hope that the external deficiencies we have encountered in the world as would-be men (the absent father, the immature father, the lack of meaningful ritual process, the scarcity of ritual elders) can be corrected. And we have not only hope but actual experience as clinicians and as individuals of inner resources not imagined by psychology before Jung. It is our experience that deep within every man are blueprints, what we can also call "hard wiring," for the calm and positive mature masculine. Jungians refer to these masculine potentials as archetypes, or "primordial images."

Jung and his successors have found that on the level of the deep unconscious the psyche of every person is grounded in what Jung called the "collective unconscious," made up of instinctual patterns and energy configurations probably inherited genetically throughout the generations of our species. These archetypes provide the very foundations of our behaviors—our thinking, our feeling, and our characteristic human reactions. They are the image makers that artists and poets and religious prophets are so close to. Jung related them directly to the instincts in other animals.

Most of us are familiar with the fact that baby ducks soon after they are hatched attach themselves to whomever or whatever is walking by at the time. This phenomenon is called imprinting. It means that the newly hatched duckling is wired for "mother," or "caretaker." It doesn't have to learn—from the outside, as it were—what a caretaker is. The archetype for caretaker comes on line shortly after the duckling comes into this world. Unfortunately, however, the "mother" the duckling meets in those first moments may not be adequate to the task of taking care of it. Nonetheless, although those in the outer world may not live up to the instinctual expectation (they may not even be ducks!), the archetype for caretaker forms the duckling's behavior.

In a similar way, human beings are wired for "mother" and "father" and many other human relationships, as well as all forms of the human experience of the world. And though those in the outer world may not live up to the archetypal expectation, the archetype is nonetheless present. It is constant and universal in all of us. We, like the duckling that mistakes a cat for its mother, mistake our actual parents for the ideal patterns and potentials within us.

Archetypal patterns gone awry, skewed into the negative by disastrous encounters with living people in the outer world—that is, in most cases, by inadequate or hostile parents—manifest in our lives as crippling psychological problems. If our parents were, as the psychologist D. W. Winnicott says, "good enough," then we are enabled to experience and access the inner blueprints for human relations in a positive way. Sadly, many of us, perhaps the majority, did not receive good enough parenting.

The existence of the archetypes is well documented by mountains of clinical evidence from the dreams and daydreams of patients, and from careful observation of entrenched patterns of human behavior. It is also documented by in-depth studies of mythology the world over. Again and again we see the same essential figures appearing in folklore and mythology. And these just happen to appear also in the dreams of people who have no knowledge of these fields. The dying-resurrecting young God, for example, is found in the myths of such diverse people as Christians, Moslem Persians, ancient Sumerians, and modern Native Americans, as well as in the dreams of those undergoing psychotherapy. The evidence is great that there are underlying patterns that determine human cognitive and emotional life.

These blueprints appear to be great in number, and they manifest themselves as both male and female. There are archetypes that pattern the thoughts and feelings and relationships of women, and there are archetypes that pattern the thoughts and feelings and relationships of men. In addition, Jungians have found that in every man there is a feminine subpersonality called the Anima, made up of the feminine archetypes. And in every woman there is a masculine subpersonality called the Animus, made up of the masculine archetypes. All human beings can access the archetypes, to a greater or lesser degree. We do this, in fact, in our interrelating with one another.

This whole field is being actively discussed and continually revised as our knowledge about the inner instinctual human world moves forward. We are just beginning to sort out in a systematic way the inner human world that has always manifested itself to us in myth, ritual, dreams, and visions. The field of archetypal psychology is in its infancy. We want to show men how they can access these positive archetypal potentials for their own benefit and for the benefit of all those around them, maybe even for the planet.

3.   *Boy Psychology*

The drug dealer, the ducking and diving political leader, the wife beater, the chronically "crabby" boss, the "hot shot" junior executive, the unfaithful husband, the company "yes man," the indifferent graduate school adviser, the "holier than thou" minister, the gang member, the father who can never find the time to attend his daughter's school programs, the coach who ridicules his star athletes, the therapist who unconsciously attacks his clients' "shining" and seeks a kind of gray normalcy for them, the yuppie—all these men have something in common. They are all boys pretending to be men. They got that way honestly, because nobody showed them what a mature man is like. Their kind of "manhood" is a pretense to manhood that goes largely undetected as such by most of us. We are continually mistaking this man's controlling, threatening, and hostile behaviors for strength. In reality, he is showing an underlying extreme vulnerability and weakness, the vulnerability of the wounded boy.

The devastating fact is that most men are fixated at an immature level of development. These early developmental levels are governed by the inner blueprints appropriate to boyhood. When they are allowed to rule what should be adulthood, when the archetypes of boyhood are not built upon and transcended by the Ego's appropriate accessing of the archetypes of mature masculinity, they cause us to act out of our hidden (to us, but seldom to others) boyishness.

We often talk with affection about boyishness in our culture. The truth is that the boy in each of us—when he is in his appropriate place in our lives—is the source of playfulness, of pleasure, of fun, of energy, of a kind of open-mindedness, that is ready for adventure and for the future. But there is another kind of boyishness that remains infantile in our interactions within ourselves and with others when manhood is required.

The Structure of the Archetypes

Each of the archetypal energy potentials in the male psyche—in both its immature and its mature forms—has a triune, or three-part, structure (see fig. 1).

At the top of the triangle is the archetype in its fullness. At the bottom of the triangle the archetype is experienced in what we call a bipolar dysfunctional, or shadow, form. In both its immature and mature forms (that is, in both Boy psychology and Man psychology terms), this bipolar dysfunction can be thought of as immature in that it represents a psychological condition that is not integrated or cohesive. Lack of cohesion in the psyche is always a symptom of inadequate development. As the personality of the boy and then the man matures into its appropriate stage of development, the poles of these shadow forms become integrated and unified.

Some boys seem more "mature" than others; they are accessing, no doubt unconsciously, the archetypes of boyhood more fully than are their peers. These boys have achieved a level of integration and inner unity that others have not. Other boys may seem more "immature," even taking into account the natural immaturity of boyhood. For example, it is right for a boy to feel the heroic within himself, to see himself as a hero. But many boys cannot do this and become caught in the bipolar shadow forms of the Hero—the Grandstander Bully or the Coward.

Different archetypes come on line at different developmental stages. The first archetype of the immature masculine to "power up" is the Divine Child. The Precocious Child and the Oedipal Child are next; the last stage of boyhood is governed by the Hero. Human development does not always proceed so neatly, of course; there are mixtures of the archetypal influences all along the way.

Interestingly, each of the archetypes of Boy psychology gives rise in a complex way to each of the archetypes of mature masculinity: the boy is father to the man. Thus, the Divine Child, modulated and enriched by life's experiences, becomes the King; the Precocious Child becomes the Magician; the Oedipal Child becomes the Lover; and the Hero becomes the Warrior.

The four archetypes of boyhood, each with a triangular structure, can be put together to form a pyramid (see fig. 2) that depicts the structure of the boy's emerging identity, his immature masculine Self. The same is true of the structure of the mature masculine Self.

As we have suggested, the adult man does not lose his boyishness, and the archetypes that form boyhood's foundation do not go away. Since archetypes cannot disappear, the mature man transcends the masculine powers of boyhood, building upon them rather than demolishing them. The resulting structure of the mature masculine Self, therefore, is a pyramid over a pyramid (see fig. 3). Though images should not be taken too literally, we are arguing that pyramids are universal symbols of the human Self.*

The Divine Child

The first, the most primal, of the immature masculine energies is the Divine Child. We are all familiar with the Christian story of the birth of the baby Jesus. He is a mystery. He comes from the Divine Realm, born of a virgin woman. Miraculous things and events attend him: the star, the worshiping shepherds, the wise men from Persia. Surrounded by his worshipers, he occupies the central place not only in the stable but in the universe. Even the animals, in popular Christmas songs, attend him. In the pictures, he radiates light, haloed by the soft, glistening straw he lies upon. Because he is God, he is almighty. At the same time,

---

* We theorize that the Self-structure in women is also pyramidal in form, and that when the pyramids of the masculine Self and the feminine Self are placed end to end, they form an octahedron, an image that graphically represents the Jungian Self, which embraces both masculine and feminine qualities. See C. G. Jung's *Aion*, translated by R. F. C. Hull, Bollingen Series XX (Princeton: Princeton Univ. Press, 1959). We have gone beyond Jung in decoding the "double quaternio."

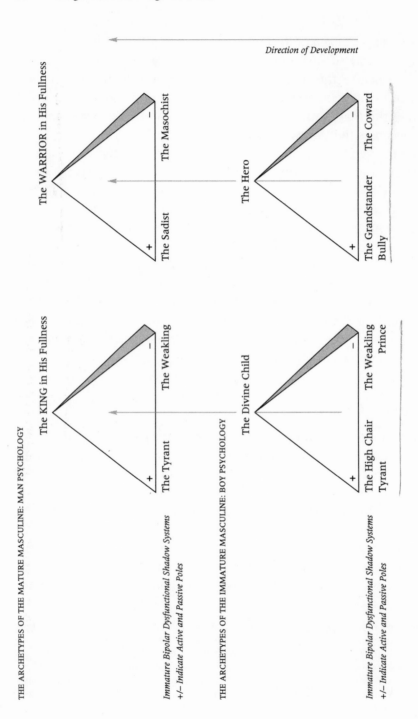

Direction of Development

THE ARCHETYPES OF THE MATURE MASCULINE: MAN PSYCHOLOGY

The WARRIOR in His Fullness

The Masochist

The Sadist

The Hero

The Grandstander Bully

The Coward

The KING in His Fullness

The Weakling

The Tyrant

Immature Bipolar Dysfunctional Shadow Systems
+/– Indicate Active and Passive Poles

THE ARCHETYPES OF THE IMMATURE MASCULINE: BOY PSYCHOLOGY

The Divine Child

The Weakling Prince

The High Chair Tyrant

Immature Bipolar Dysfunctional Shadow Systems
+/– Indicate Active and Passive Poles

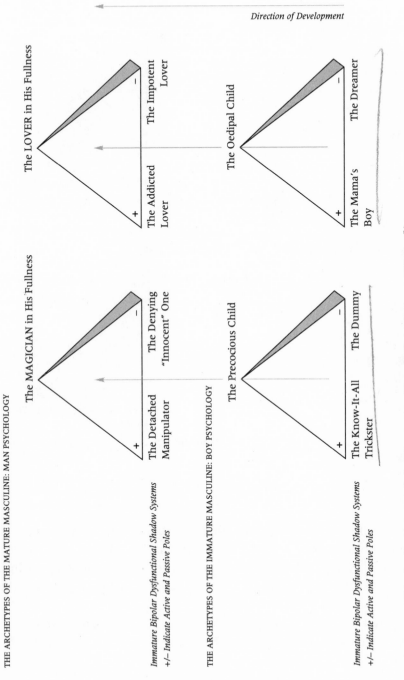

THE ARCHETYPES OF THE MATURE MASCULINE: MAN PSYCHOLOGY

The MAGICIAN in His Fullness

The Detached Manipulator

The Denying "Innocent" One

The LOVER in His Fullness

The Addicted Lover

The Impotent Lover

Immature Bipolar Dysfunctional Shadow Systems
+/– Indicate Active and Passive Poles

THE ARCHETYPES OF THE IMMATURE MASCULINE: BOY PSYCHOLOGY

The Precocious Child

The Know-It-All Trickster

The Dummy

The Oedipal Child

The Mama's Boy

The Dreamer

Immature Bipolar Dysfunctional Shadow Systems
+/– Indicate Active and Passive Poles

Direction of Development

Figure 1. The Archetypes of the Immature and the Mature Masculine

THE PYRAMIDAL STRUCTURE OF THE MATURE MASCULINE SELF

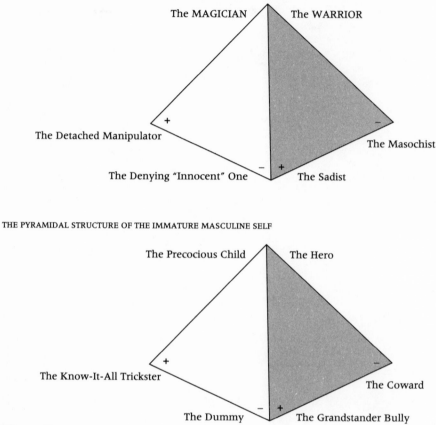

Figure 2.

he is totally vulnerable and helpless. No sooner is he born than the evil King Herod sniffs him out and seeks to kill him. He must be protected and spirited away to Egypt until he can be strong enough to begin his life's work and until the forces that would destroy him have spent their energy.

What is not often realized is that this myth does not stand alone. The religions of the world are rich with stories of the miraculous Baby

THE PYRAMIDAL STRUCTURE OF THE MATURE MASCULINE SELF

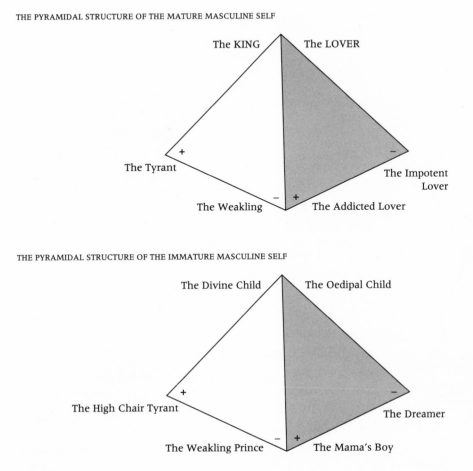

THE PYRAMIDAL STRUCTURE OF THE IMMATURE MASCULINE SELF

Boy. The Christian story itself is modeled in part on the story of the birth of the great Persian prophet Zoroaster, complete with miracles in nature, magi, and threats on his life. In Judaism, there is the story of the baby Moses born to be the deliverer of his people, to be the Great Teacher and the Mediator between God and human beings. He was raised as a prince of Egypt. And yet, in his first days, his life was threatened by an edict from the pharaoh, and he was placed, helpless

THE LAYERED PYRAMID, OR THE PYRAMID WITHIN A PYRAMID,
OF THE MASCULINE SELF STRUCTURES

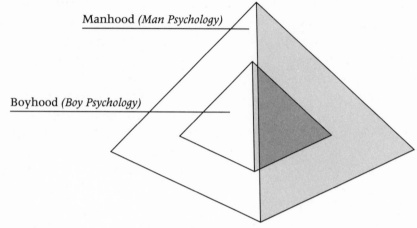

Manhood *(Man Psychology)*

Boyhood *(Boy Psychology)*

Figure 3.

and vulnerable, in a reed basket and set adrift on the Nile. The model for this story was the much older legend of the infancy of the great Mesopotamian king Sargon of Akkad. And from all over the world we hear legends about the wondrous infancy of the baby Buddha, the baby Krishna, the baby Dionysus.

Even less known is that this figure of the Divine Baby Boy, universal in our religions, is also universal inside ourselves. This can be seen from the dreams of men in psychoanalysis, who frequently, especially as they start to get better, dream about a Baby Boy who fills the dream with light and joy and a sense of wonder and refreshment. Often, too, when a man in therapy starts to feel better, the urge comes to him, perhaps for the first time in his life, to have children.

These events are signals that something new and creative, fresh and "innocent," is being born within him. A new phase of his life is beginning. Creative parts of himself that he had been unconscious of are now thrusting upward into awareness. He is experiencing new life. But whenever the Divine Child within us makes itself known, attack from the Herods, within and without, is not far behind. New life, including new psychological life, is always fragile. When we feel this new energy manifesting within us we need to move to protect it, because it is going to be attacked. A man may say in his therapy, "I may actually be getting better!" And right away, he may be answered by an inner voice that says, "Oh no, you're not. You know you can never be well." It is then time to get the fragile Divine Child to "Egypt."

Picking up on the theme in the Christmas story of the adoring animals and the angels' proclamation of peace on earth, we can see in the Greek myth of Orpheus that the Divine Child is the archetypal energy that prefigures the mature masculine energy of the King. The man-God Orpheus sits at the center of the world playing his lyre and singing a song that brings all the animals of the forest to him. They are drawn by the song, prey and predator. And they come together around Orpheus in perfect harmony, their differences resolved, all of the opposites brought together into a world-transcending order (characteristic functions of the King, as we shall see).

But this theme of the Divine Child bringing peace and order to the whole world, including the animal world (and animals, looked at psychologically, stand for our own often conflicting instincts), is not limited to ancient myths. A young man who had entered analysis once told us a story about an unusual event in his childhood. When he was probably five or six years old, he told us, he went out into his backyard one spring afternoon yearning for something he was too young to identify but that, upon reflection later in life, he saw was a yearning for inner peace and harmony and a sense of oneness with all things. He stood with his back to a huge oak tree which grew in his yard, and he began to sing a song he made up as he went along. It was hypnotic for him. He sang his longing. He sang his sadness. And he sang a kind of minor-key deep joy. He sang a song of compassion for all living things. It was a kind of self- and other-soothing lullaby (a song to the Baby Boy). And pretty soon he began to notice that birds were coming to the tree, a few at a time. He continued singing, and as he sang, more birds came, whirling and circling around the tree and alighting in its branches. At last, the tree was filled with birds. It was alive with them.

It seemed to him that they had been lured by the beauty and compassion of his song. They confirmed *his* beauty, and answered *his* yearning by coming to adore him. The tree became a Tree of Life, and refreshed by this confirmation of his inner Divine Child, he could go on.

The Divine Child archetype that appears in our myths as Orpheus, as Christ, as the infant Moses, and as various figures in the myths of many religions, in the dreams of men undergoing therapy, and in the actual experiences of boys appears to be in the "hard wiring" of us all. We seem to be born with it. It goes by many names and is evaluated differently by the different schools of psychology. Usually, psychologists condemn it and, in effect, try to disconnect their clients from it. The important thing is to see that the Divine Child is built into us as a primal pattern of the immature masculine.

Freud talked about it as the Id, the "It." He saw it as the "primitive" or "infantile" drives, amoral, forceful, and full of God-like pretensions. It was the underlying push of impersonal Nature itself, concerned only with satisfying the unlimited needs of the child.

The psychologist Alfred Adler talked about it as the hidden "power drive" in each of us, as the hidden superiority complex that covers our real sense of vulnerability, weakness, and inferiority. (Remember, the Divine Child is both all-powerful, the center of the universe, and at the same time totally helpless and weak. In fact, this is the actual experience of infants.)

Heinz Kohut, who developed what he called "self-psychology," talks about it as "the grandiose self organization," which is demanding of ourselves and others in ways that can never be fulfilled. The most recent psychoanalytic theory suggests that people who are possessed by or identified with this "infantile" grandiosity are expressing a "narcissistic personality disorder."

The followers of Carl Jung, however, view this Divine Child differently. They do not see it in largely pathological terms. Jungians believe that the Divine Child is a vital aspect of the Archetypal Self—the Self with a capital *S*, because it is different from the Ego, which is the self with a small *s*. For Jungians, this Divine Child within us is the source of life. It possesses magical, empowering qualities, and getting in touch with it produces an enormous sense of well-being, enthusiasm for life, and great peace and joy, as it did for the young boy under the oak tree.

These differing schools of psychoanalysis, we believe, are each right. Each picks up on the two different aspects of this energy—the one integrated and unified, and the other the shadow side. At the top of the triangular archetypal structure, we experience the Divine Child, who renews us and keeps us "young at heart." At the base of the triangle, we experience what we call the High Chair Tyrant and the Weakling Prince.

The High Chair Tyrant

The High Chair Tyrant is epitomized by the image of Little Lord Faun-tleroy sitting in his high chair, banging his spoon on the tray, and screaming for his mother to feed him, kiss him, and attend him. Like a dark version of the Christ child, he is the center of the universe; others exist to meet his all-powerful needs and desires. But when the food comes, it often does not meet his specifications: it's not good enough; it's not the right kind; it's too hot or too cold, too sweet or too sour. So he spits it on the floor or throws it across the room. If he becomes suffi-ciently self-righteous, no food, no matter how hungry he is, will be adequate. And if his mother picks him up after "failing" him so com-pletely, he will scream and twist and reject her advances, because they were not offered at exactly the right moment. The High Chair Tyrant hurts himself with his grandiosity—the limitlessness of his demands—because he rejects the very things that he needs for life: food and love.

Characteristics of the High Chair Tyrant include arrogance (what the Greeks called hubris, or overweening pride), childishness (in the negative sense), and irresponsibility, even to himself as a mortal infant who has to meet his biological and psychological needs. All of this is what psychologists call inflation or pathological narcissism. The High Chair Tyrant needs to learn that he is not the center of the universe and that the universe does not exist to fulfill his every need, or, better put, his limitless needs, his pretensions to godhood. It will nurture him, but not in his form as God.

The High Chair Tyrant, through the Shadow King, may continue to be a ruling archetypal influence in adulthood. We all know the story of the promising leader, the CEO, or the presidential candidate, who starts to rise to great prominence and then shoots himself in the foot. He sabotages his success, and crashes to the earth. The ancient Greeks said that hubris is always followed by nemesis. The gods always bring down those mortals who get too arrogant, demanding, or inflated. Icarus, for instance, made wings of feathers and wax in order to fly like the birds (read "gods") and then in his inflation, and against his father's warning, flew too close to the sun. The sun melted the wax, the wings disintegrated, and he plummeted into the sea.

We are familiar with the saying "Power corrupts, and absolute power corrupts absolutely." King Louis XVI of France lost his head because of his arrogance. Often as we men rise in the corporate structure, as we gain more and more authority and power, the risk of self-destruction also rises. The boss who wants only yes men, who doesn't want to know what's going on, the president who doesn't want to hear his generals' advice, the school principal who can't tolerate criticism from his teachers—all are men possessed by the High Chair Tyrant riding for a fall.

The High Chair Tyrant who attacks his human host is the perfectionist; he expects the impossible of himself and berates himself (just as his mother did) when he can't meet the demands of the infant within. The Tyrant pressures a man for more and better performance and is never satisfied with what he produces. The unfortunate man becomes the slave (as the mother was) of the grandiose two-year-old inside of him. He has to have more material things. He can't make mistakes. And because he can't possibly meet the demands of the inner Tyrant, he develops ulcers and gets sick. He can't, in the end, stand up to the unrelenting pressure. We men often deal with the Tyrant by finally having a heart attack. We go on strike against him. Finally, the only way to escape the Little Lord is to die.

When the High Chair Tyrant cannot be brought under control, he will manifest in a Stalin, Caligula, or Hitler—all malignant sociopaths. We will become the CEO who would rather see the company fail than deal with his own grandiosity, his own identification with the demanding "god" within. We can be Little Hitlers, but we're going to destroy our country in the process.

It has been said that the Divine Child wants just to be and to have all things flow toward him. He does not want to do. The artist wants to be admired without having to lift a finger. The CEO wants to sit in his office, enjoying his leather chairs, his cigars, and his attractive secretaries, drawing his high salary, and enjoying his perks. But he does not want to do anything for the company. He imagines himself invulnerable and all-important. He often demeans and degrades others who are trying to accomplish something. He is in his high chair, and he is setting himself up to get the ax.

The Weakling Prince

The other side of the bipolar shadow of the Divine Child is the Weakling Prince. The boy (and later, the man) who is possessed by the Weakling Prince appears to have very little personality, no enthusiasm for life, and very little initiative. This is the boy who needs to be coddled, who dictates to those around him by his silent or his whining and complaining helplessness. He needs to be carried around on a pillow. Everything is too much for him. He rarely joins in children's games; he has few friends; he doesn't do well in school; he is frequently hypochondriacal; his slightest wish is his parents' command; the entire family system revolves around his comfort. He reveals the dishonesty of his helplessness, however, in his daggerlike verbal assaults on his siblings, his biting sarcasm directed against them, and his patent manipulation of their feelings. Because he has convinced his parents that he is a helpless victim of life and that others are picking on him, when a controversy arises between himself and a sibling, his parents tend to punish the sibling and excuse him.

The Weakling Prince is the polar opposite of the High Chair Tyrant, and though he rarely throws the tantrums of the Tyrant, he nonetheless occupies a less easily detectable throne. As is the case with all bipolar disorders, the Ego possessed by one pole will, from time to time, gradually slide or suddenly jump over to the other pole. Using the imagery of bipolar magnetism to describe this phenomenon, we can say that the polarity of the magnet reverses depending on the direction of an electrical current passing through it. When such a reversal occurs in the boy caught in the bipolar shadow of the Divine Child, he will switch from tyrannical outbursts to depressed passivity, or from apparent weakness to rageful displays.

Accessing the Divine Child

In order to access the Divine Child appropriately, we need to acknowledge him, but not identify with him. We need to love and admire the creativity and beauty of this primal aspect of the masculine Self, because if we don't have this connection with him, we are never going to see the possibilities in life. We are never going to seize opportunities for newness and freshness.

Whether activist, artist, administrator, or teacher, everyone in a leadership capacity needs to be connected with the creative, playful Child in order to manifest his full potential and advance his cause, his company, and generativity and creativity in himself and others. Connection with this archetype keeps us from feeling washed up, bored, and unable to see the abundance of human potential all around us.

We have said that therapists often depreciate the grandiose Self within their clients. Although it is necessary, at times, for clients to gain emotional and cognitive distance from the Divine Child, we ourselves have not encountered many men (at least among those who seek therapy) who *identify* with their creativity. Rather, they usually need to get in touch with it. We want to *encourage* greatness in men. We want to encourage ambition. We believe that nobody really wants to be sort of gray-normal. Often, the definition of normal is "average." We live, it seems to us, in an age under the curse of normalcy, characterized by the elevation of the mediocre. It seems likely that therapists who persistently depreciate the "shining" of the grandiose Self in their clients are themselves split off from their own Divine Child. They are envying the beauty and freshness, the creativity and vitality, of the Child in their clients.

The ancient Romans believed that every human baby is born with what they called his or her "genius," a guardian spirit assigned at birth.

Roman birthday parties were held not so much to honor an individual as to honor that person's genius, the divine being that came into the world with him or her. The Romans knew that it was not the man's Ego that was the source of his music, his art, his statecraft, or his courageous deeds. It was the Divine Child, an aspect of the Self within him.

We need to ask ourselves two questions. The first one is not *whether* we are manifesting the High Chair Tyrant or the Weakling Prince but *how*—because we all are manifesting both to some extent and in some form. At the very least, we all do this when we regress into our Child when we are fatigued or extremely frightened. The second question is not whether the creative Child exists in us but how we are honoring him or not honoring him. If we're not feeling him in our personal lives and in our work, then we have to ask ourselves how we are blocking him.

The Precocious Child

There is a wonderful statuette of the ancient Egyptian magician and vizier, Imhotep, as a boy. Imhotep is sitting on a little throne reading a scroll. His face is gentle and thoughtful, but alive with an inner glow. His eyes look down at the written word that he holds reverently in his hands. His posture shows grace, poise, concentration, and self-confidence. Not a true portrait, this statuette is really an image of the archetype of the Precocious Child.

The Precocious Child manifests in a boy when he is eager to learn, when his mind is quickened, when he wants to share what he is learning with others. There's a glint in his eye and an energy of body and mind that shows he is adventuring in the world of ideas. This boy (and later, the man) wants to know the "why" of everything. He asks his parents, "Why is the sky blue?" "Why do the leaves fall?" "Why do things have to die?" He wants to know the "how" of things, the "what," and the "where." He often learns to read at an early age so that he can answer his own questions. He's usually a good student and an eager participant in class discussions. Often this boy is also talented in one or more areas: he may be able to draw and paint well or play a musical instrument with proficiency. He may also be good at sports. The Precocious Child is the source of so-called child prodigies.

The Precocious Child is the origin of our curiosity and our adventurous impulses. He urges us to be explorers and pioneers of the unknown, the strange and mysterious. He causes us to wonder at the world *around* us and the world *inside* us. A boy for whom the Precocious Child is a powerful influence wants to know what makes other people tick as well as what makes himself tick. He wants to know why people act the way they do, why he has the feelings he has. He tends to be introverted and reflective, and he is able to see the hidden connections in things. He can achieve cognitive detachment from the people around him long before his peers are able to accomplish this. Though introverted and reflective, he is also extroverted and eagerly reaches out to others to share his insights and his talents with them. He often experiences a powerful urge to help others with his knowledge, and his friends often come to him for a shoulder to cry on as well as for help with their schoolwork. The Precocious Child in a man keeps his sense of wonder and curiosity alive, stimulates his intellect, and moves him in the direction of the mature magician.

The Know-It-All Trickster

The bipolar Shadow of the Precocious Child, like all the shadow forms of the archetypes of the immature masculine, can be carried over into adulthood, where it causes would-be men to manifest inappropriate infantilism in their thoughts, feelings, and behaviors. The Know-It-All Trickster is, as the name implies, that immature masculine energy that plays tricks, of a more or less serious nature, in one's own life and on others. He is expert at creating appearances, and then "selling" us on those appearances. He seduces people into believing him, and then he pulls the rug out from under them. He gets us to believe in him, to trust him, and then he betrays us and laughs at our misery. He leads us to a paradise in the jungle, only to serve us a feast of cyanide. He's always looking for a sucker. He is the practical joker, adept at making fools of us. He is a manipulator.

The Know-It-All is that aspect of the Trickster in a boy or a man that enjoys intimidating others. The boy (or man) under the power of the Know-It-All shoots off his mouth a lot. He's always got his hand up in class, not because he wants to participate in the discussion, but because he wants his classmates to understand that he is more intelligent than they are. He wants to trick them into believing that, compared to him, they are dolts.

The boy possessed by the Know-It-All, however, does not necessarily limit his exaggerated precociousness to intellectual showmanship. He may be a know-it-all about any subject or activity. A boy from a wealthy English family came to the United States one summer to spend a month in a YMCA camp. He spent much of his time telling the other boys, whom he called plebes, all about his many travels in Europe and Asia with his diplomat father. When the other boys asked about details of this or that foreign city, the English boy would respond with, "You stupid Americans. The only thing you know about is your cornfields!" And he performed his "I'm superior to you" show in a British upper-crust accent. Needless to say, the American boys felt ashamed and angry.

The boy or man under the power of the Know-It-All makes many enemies. He is verbally abusive of others, whom he regards as his inferiors. As a result, in grade school, he can often be found on the bottom of a pile of angry boys who are whacking away at him. He comes away from these encounters with black eyes, but with a defiant conviction of his own superiority. In one extreme case that we know of, the Know-It-All boy came to believe that he was the Second Coming of Jesus Christ. The only thing he couldn't figure out was why no one seemed to recognize him.

The Know-It-All man who is still possessed by this infantile shadow form of the Precocious Child wears his superiority in his suspenders and in his business suits, carries it in his briefcase, and displays it in his "I'm too busy and too important to talk with you now" attitude. He's characteristically smug, and often wears a cocky grin. He frequently dominates conversations, turning friendly discussions into lectures and arguments into diatribes. He depreciates those who don't know what he knows or hold opinions that differ from his. Because the Trickster is the umbrella complex under which the Know-It-All operates, the man caught in this infantile influence is usually deceiving others—and perhaps himself as well—about the depth of his knowledge or the level of his importance.

But he also has a positive side. He is very good at deflating Egos, our own and those of others. And often we need deflating. He can spot, in an instant, when, and in exactly what way, we are inflated and identified with our grandiosity. And he goes for it, in order to reduce us to human size and expose to us all of our frailties. This was the role of the Fool in the kings' courts of medieval Europe. When everyone else at a great ceremony was adoring the king, and the king himself was beginning to adore the king, the Fool would caper into the middle of the ceremonies, and—fart! He was saying, "Don't get inflated. All of us here are only human beings, no matter what status we accord each other."

Jesus in the Bible calls Satan the Father of Lies, thus identifying Satan with the Trickster in his negative aspect. However, in a roundabout way the Bible also shows Satan, the Trickster, in a positive light, though most of us have probably missed this. The story of Job, for instance, depicts a relationship of mutual respect between Job and God. God has given Job great wealth and material security, health, and a large family. Job, for his part, ceaselessly praises God. It's a mutual admiration society. Then in comes Satan, sniffing out the hypocrisy in the whole thing. He's a troublemaker—for the sake of truth. His idea is that if God curses Job, Job will eventually stop singing the Lord's praises. God doesn't want to believe Satan, but he goes along with the plan, probably instinctively knowing that Satan is right. And he is! Once God has taken away everything Job had—his family, his wealth, his health—Job finally throws off his superficial piety, shakes his fist at God, and rips him up one side and down the other. God responds by intimidating Job.

Even in the story of the Garden of Eden, Satan makes trouble for the sake of exposing the fraudulent and delusional nature of the supposedly "good" creation. God wanted to believe that everything he had made was good, but then, after all, he had made evil and hung it on the

Tree of the Knowledge of Good and Evil. Satan, in the form of the serpent, was determined to expose the shadow side of this "all-good" creation. He succeeded through the "fall" of Adam and Eve. Only after Satan had exposed the evil in creation—and, by implication, in the Creator—could honesty and healing begin.

The young gang members in *West Side Story,* who in a clowning and tricksterish way try to make excuses for themselves and their destructive behavior to their mock-up Officer Krupke, are actually, and quite accurately, exposing the shadow side, the less than idyllic side, of the society that made them what they are.

How does the Trickster work? Let's say that you are preparing to give what you regard as the most brilliant presentation of your life. You're so proud of your special insights! You sit down at the computer and order it to print out the notes you had put into it earlier, and the printer doesn't work. Your own inner Trickster has tricked you.

Or you're going to make an appearance at an important function. You're timing it so that you know everyone will be waiting for you—just for a few minutes, just long enough for them to realize how important you are. You go to the car at last, preparing to make your triumphal journey. And you can't find your keys. There they are, locked in the car, still in the ignition. Hubris leads to nemesis. This is how the Trickster works against (in the long run, perhaps, *for*) us.

But he works, through us, against others too. Maybe you're the practical joker, mercilessly hounding others with your pranks until someone does you one better and you are forced to realize how much it hurts. You're the car salesman who cheats your customers on the true markup of the car—and then management cheats *you* on your commission.

We once knew a graduate student who was really possessed by this aspect of the archetype. He couldn't stop exposing others' weaknesses through his charming, and not so charming, humor at their expense. He laughed at his professors' blunders in the classroom. He laughed when the president of the school stumbled over his words. He himself had political aspirations, hoping to create a student movement for his favorite cause. But he alienated the very people he needed as supporters and mentors. His tricksterish behavior finally isolated him and left him powerless. It was only afterward, in therapy, when he had made himself familiar with the possessing force of this archetype, by studying Native American portrayals of the Trickster, that he was able to free himself of his compulsive and self-destructive behavior.

Perhaps the most familiar Trickster is in the Bible, in the story of Jacob and Esau and how Jacob got Esau's birthright through "selling" him a bowl of soup. Jacob tricked his older brother into giving up all his rightful status and wealth as the heir to their father's fortune. Through manipulation, he took what was not his.

We need to clearly understand this immature energy. Though its purpose in its positive mode seems to be to expose lies, if it is left unchecked, it moves into its negative side and becomes destructive of oneself and others. For the negative side of this immature masculine energy is really hostile and deprecating of all the real effort, all the rights, all the beauty of others. The Trickster, like the High Chair Tyrant, does not want to do anything himself. He does not want to honestly earn anything. He just wants to be, and to be what he has no right to be. He is, in psychological language, passive-aggressive.

This is the energy form that seeks the fall of great men, that delights in the destruction of a man of importance. But the Trickster does not want to replace the man who has fallen. He does not want to take up that man's responsibilities. In fact, he doesn't want any responsibilities. He wants to do just enough to wreck things for others.

The Trickster causes a boy (or a boyish man) to have an authority problem. Such a boy (or man) can always find a man to hate him and eventually shoot him down. He will readily believe that all men in power are corrupt and abusive. But, like the man possessed by the Weakling Prince, he is condemned forever to be on the outskirts of life, never able to take responsibility for himself or his actions.

His energy comes from envy. The less a man is in touch with his true talents and abilities, the more he will envy others. If we envy a lot, we are denying our own realistic greatness, our own Divine Child. What we need to do, then, is to get in touch with our own specialness, our own beauty, and our own creativity. Envy blocks creativity.

The Trickster is the archetype that rushes in to fill the vacuum in the immature man or boy left by the boy's denial of and lack of connection with the Divine Child. The Trickster gets activated developmentally within us when we have been depreciated and attacked by our parents (or older siblings), when we have been emotionally abused. If we don't feel our real specialness, we will come under the power of the Trickster, the "Know-It-All," and deflate others' sense of their specialness, even when such deflation is not called for. The Know-It-All Trickster has no heroes, because to have heroes is to admire others. We can only admire others if we have a sense of our own worthiness, and a developing sense of security about our own creative energies.

The Dummy

The boy (or man) who is under the power of the other pole of the dys-functional Shadow of the Precocious Child, the naive Dummy, like the Weakling Prince, lacks personality, vigor, and creativity. He seems unresponsive and dull. He can't seem to learn his multiplication tables, count change, or tell time. He is frequently labeled a slow learner. In addition, he lacks a sense of humor and frequently seems to miss the point of jokes. He may appear to be physically inept as well. His coordination is off, so he often becomes the butt of ridicule and contempt when he fumbles the ball on the playing field or strikes out in the last of the ninth. This boy may also appear to be naive. He is, or seems to be, the last kid on the block to learn about the "birds and the bees."

The Dummy's ineptitude, however, is frequently less than honest. He may grasp far more than he shows, and his duncelike behavior may mask a hidden grandiosity that feels itself too important (as well as too vulnerable) to come into the world. Thus, intimately intertwined with a secret Know-It-All, the Dummy is also a Trickster.

The Oedipal Child

All the immature masculine energies are overly tied, one way or another, to Mother, and are deficient in their experience of the nurtur-ing and mature masculine.

Although the boy for whom the Oedipal Child is a powerful arche-typal influence may be deficient in his experience of the nurturing mas-culine, he is able to access the positive qualities of the archetype. He is passionate and has a sense of wonder and a deep appreciation for con-nectedness with his inner depths, with others, and with all things. He is warm, related, and affectionate. He also expresses, through his expe-rience of connectedness to Mother (the primal relationship for almost all of us), the origins of what we can call spirituality. His sense of the mystic oneness and mutual communion of all things comes out of his deep yearning for the infinitely nurturing, infinitely good, infinitely beautiful Mother.

This Mother is not his real, mortal mother. *She* is bound to disap-point him much of the time in his need for connectedness and perfect, or infinite, love and nurturing. Rather, the Mother that he is sensing beyond his own, beyond all the beauty and feeling (what the Greeks called *eros*) in the things of the world, and that he is experiencing in the deep feelings and images of his inner life is the Great Mother—the God-dess in her many forms in the myths and legends of many peoples and cultures.

A young man who once came into analysis in part because he was trying to work through his mother issues reported a remarkable insight that his own unconscious handed him. About halfway through his analysis, while visiting his mother, he and she got into one of their fre-quent quarrels. He could not get her to see his point. And he blurted out in disgust, "God, All-Mother, Mighty!" It was a Freudian slip, as we say. He had meant to say, "God Almighty, Mother!" He and his mother were stopped cold in their argument. Both were embarrassed and laughed nervously, because both realized the significance of his slip of the tongue. From that moment on, he began to direct his spiritual sense of the All-Mother, Mighty, toward the archetypal Great Mother, who, he realized with an inner conviction, was the Mother of his own mortal mother. He began to stop experiencing his mother as the Great Mother and began to be able to relieve her, and all other women, from carrying so heavy a burden as God-likeness for him. Not only did his relation-ships with his girlfriend and his mother improve, but his spirituality began to deepen significantly. He began to turn his sense of deep relatedness into spiritual gold.

The Mama's Boy

The Oedipal Child's Shadow consists of the Mama's Boy and the Dreamer. The Mama's Boy is, as we all know, "tied to Mama's apron strings." He causes a boy to fantasize about marrying his mother, about taking her away from his father. If there is no father, or a weak father, this so-called Oedipal urge comes on all the stronger, and this crippling side of the Oedipal Child's bipolar Shadow may possess him.

The term Oedipus complex comes from Freud, who saw in the legend of the Greek king Oedipus a mythological account of this immature masculine energy form. The story is familiar.

King Laertes and his wife, Jocasta, had a baby boy whom they named Oedipus. Because of a prophecy that said that Oedipus would grow up to kill his father, Laertes had this special child taken out into the country and exposed on a hillside, where, it was assumed, the elements would kill him. However, as is always the case with Divine Boys, Oedipus was rescued. He was found by a shepherd and raised to manhood.

One day, as Oedipus was walking along a country road, a chariot nearly ran him down. He got into a fight with the owner of the chariot and killed him. The chariot's owner, unbeknownst to him, was his father Laertes. Oedipus then went on to Thebes, where he learned that the queen was seeking a husband. The queen was Jocasta, his mother. Oedipus married her and took his father's throne. It was only years later, when blight descended upon the kingdom, that the awful truth was uncovered, and Oedipus, the wrongful king, was cast down. The underlying psychological truth in the story is that Oedipus was inflated. He was struck down by the gods for killing his father (the "god") and marrying his mother (the "goddess"). Thus, he was destroyed for the unconscious inflation of his unconscious pretensions to godhood. For every child, from a developmental point of view, Mother is the goddess and Father is the god. Boys who are too bound to the Mother get hurt.

There is also the story of Adonis, who became the lover of Aphrodite, the goddess of love. A mortal boy making claims on a goddess could not be tolerated, so Adonis was struck down by a wild boar (really, a god in animal form—the Father) and killed.

Something else happens to the Mama's Boy. He often gets caught up in chasing the beautiful, the poignant, the yearning for union with Mother from one woman to another. He can never be satisfied with a mortal woman, because what he is seeking is the immortal Goddess. Here we have the Don Juan syndrome. The Oedipal Child, inflated beyond mortal dimensions, cannot be bound to one woman.

In addition, the boy under the power of the Mama's Boy is what is called autoerotic. He may compulsively masturbate. He may be into pornography, seeking the Goddess in the nearly infinite forms of the female body. Some men under the infantile power of the Mama's Boy aspect of the Oedipal Child have vast collections of pictures of nude women, alone or making love with men. He is seeking to experience his masculinity, his phallic power, his generativity. But instead of affirming his own masculinity as a mortal man, he is really seeking to experience the penis of God—the Great Phallus—that experiences *all* women, or rather that experiences union with the Mother Goddess in her infinity of female forms.

Caught up in masturbation and the compulsive use of pornography, the Mama's Boy, like all immature energies, wants just to be. He does not want to do what it takes to actually have union with a mortal woman and to deal with all the complex feelings involved in an intimate relationship. He does not want to take responsibility.

The Dreamer

The other pole of the dysfunctional Shadow of the Oedipal Child is the Dreamer. The Dreamer takes the spiritual impulses of the Oedipal Child to an extreme. Whereas the boy possessed by the Mama's Boy also shows signs of passivity, he at least actively seeks "Mother." The Dreamer, however, causes a boy to feel isolated and cut off from all human relationships. For the boy who is under the spell of the Dreamer, relationships are with intangible things and with the world of the imagination within him. As a consequence, while other children are playing, he may sit on a rock, dreaming his dreams. He accomplishes little and appears withdrawn and depressed. Often his dreams tend to be melancholy, on the one hand, or highly idyllic and ethereal, on the other.

The boy possessed by the Dreamer, like a boy possessed by some of the other shadow poles, is less than honest, though his dishonesty is usually unconscious. His isolated, ethereal behavior may mask the hidden, and opposite, pole of the Oedipal Child's Shadow, the Mama's Boy. What this boy really shows, in a roundabout way, is his pique at failing to achieve possession of the Mother. His grandiosity in seeking to possess the Mother lies hidden by the Dreamer's depression.

The Hero

There is much confusion about the archetype of the Hero. It is generally assumed that the heroic approach to life, or to a task, is the noblest, but this is only partly true. The Hero is, in fact, only an advanced form of Boy psychology—the most advanced form, the peak, actually, of the masculine energies of the boy, the archetype that characterizes the best in the adolescent stage of development. Yet it is immature, and when it is carried over into adulthood as the governing archetype, it blocks men from full maturity.

If we think about the Hero as the Grandstander, or the Bully, this negative aspect becomes clearer.

The Grandstander Bully

The boy (or man) under the power of the Bully intends to impress others. His strategies are designed to proclaim his superiority and his right to dominate those around him. He claims center stage as his birthright. If ever his claims to special status are challenged, watch the ensuing rageful displays! He will assault those who question what they "smell" as his inflation with vicious verbal and often physical abuse. These attacks against others are aimed at staving off recognition of his underlying cowardice and his deep insecurity. The man still under the influence of this negative aspect of the Hero is not a team player. He is a loner. He's a hot-shot junior executive, salesman, revolutionary, stock market manipulator. He's the soldier who takes unnecessary risks in combat and, if he's in a position of leadership, requires the same of his men. Many a story has come out of Vietnam, for instance, about the "heroic" young officers, bucking for promotion, who often required their men to risk their lives in brave gestures. Some of these officers were "fragged" (i.e., killed) for their inflated heroic attitudes.

Another example is the character played by Tom Cruise in the movie *Top Gun*. Here was a young fighter pilot, highly motivated, who would listen to no one, a young man who had something to prove, a grandstander, who, though creative, took dangerous risks with his plane and his navigator. The universal reaction among his fellow pilots was rejection and disgust. Even his best friend, though he loved him and remained loyal to him, eventually had to confront him with how he was hurting himself and the team.

The movie is really a story about a boy becoming a man. It is only after the Cruise character accidentally contributes to the death of his navigator-friend in a tight aerial maneuver, and suffers the grief of that, and only after he loses the competition for "top gun" to the more mature "Iceman" that he begins to move from adolescence to manhood. The difference between the Hero and the mature Warrior is precisely the difference between Cruise's character and Iceman.

The man who is possessed by the Grandstander Bully pole of the Hero's Shadow has an inflated sense of his own importance and his own abilities. As a corporate executive recently told us, when confronted with the young heroes in his company, he has to tell them from time to time, "You boys are good. But you're not as good as you think you are. You will be someday. But you're not now."

The hero begins by thinking that he is invulnerable, that only the "impossible dream" is for him, that he can "fight the unbeatable foe" and win. But if the dream really is impossible, and if the foe really is unbeatable, then the hero is in for trouble.

In fact, we see this often. The sense of invulnerability, a manifestation of the Grandstander Bully and of the God-like pretensions of all these immature masculine energy forms, leaves the man under the influence of the Shadow Hero open to the danger of his own demise. He will shoot himself in the foot, in the end. The heroic General Patton, though immensely imaginative, creative, and inspiring to his troops, at least at times, sabotaged himself with his risk taking, his immature competition with the British General Montgomery, and his insightful, but boyishly brash remarks. Rather than being assigned a mission for which his true talent qualified him (to head the Allied invasion of Europe, for instance), he was sidelined precisely because he was a hero and not fully a warrior.

As is the case with the other immature masculine archetypes, the Hero is overly tied to the Mother. But the Hero has a driving need to overcome her. He is locked in mortal combat with the feminine, striving to conquer it and to assert his masculinity. In the medieval legends about heroes and damsels, we are seldom told what happens once the hero has slain the dragon and married the princess. We don't hear what happened in their marriage, because the Hero, as an archetype, doesn't know what to do with the Princess once he's won her. He doesn't know what to do when things return to normal.

The Hero's downfall is that he doesn't know and is unable to acknowledge his own limitations. A boy or a man under the power of the Shadow Hero cannot really realize that he is a mortal being. Denial of death—the ultimate limitation on human life—is his specialty.

In this connection, we might think for a moment about the heroic nature of our Western culture. Its main business seems to be, as is often said, the "conquest" of Nature, its use and manipulation. Pollution and environmental catastrophe are the increasingly obvious penalties for such a brash and immature project. The field of medicine operates on the usually unspoken assumption that disease, and eventually death itself, can be eliminated. Our modern worldview has serious difficulty facing human limitations. When we do not face our true limitations, we are inflated, and sooner or later our inflation will be called to account.

The Coward

The boy possessed by the Coward, the other pole of the Hero's bipolar Shadow, shows an extreme reluctance to stand up for himself in physical confrontations. He will usually run away from a fight, perhaps excusing himself by claiming that it is more "manly" to walk away. But he will feel wretched in spite of his excuses. It is not only physical fights he will avoid, however. He will tend to allow himself to be bullied emotionally and intellectually as well. When someone else is demanding or forceful with him, the boy under the power of the Coward—and unable to feel heroic about himself—will cave in. He will easily acquiesce to pressure from others; he will feel invaded and run-over, like a doormat. When he has had enough of this, however, the hidden grandiosity of the Grandstander Bully within him will erupt and launch a violent verbal and/or physical assault upon his "enemy," an assault for which the other is totally unprepared.

But having described the negative, or shadow, aspects of the Grandstander/Coward, we nonetheless have to ask ourselves why the Hero is present in our psyches at all. Why is this a part of our personal developmental history as men? What is the evolutionary adaptation that it serves?

What the Hero does is mobilize the boy's delicate Ego structures to enable him to break with the Mother at the end of boyhood and face the difficult tasks that life is beginning to assign him. The Hero energies call upon the boy's masculine reserves, which will be refined as he matures, in order to establish his independence and his competence, for him to be able to experience his own budding abilities, to "push the outside of the envelope" and test himself against the difficult, even hostile, forces in the world. The Hero enables him to establish a beachhead against the overwhelming power of the unconscious (much of which, for men at least, is experienced as feminine, as Mother). The Hero enables the boy to begin to assert himself and define himself as distinct from all others, so that ultimately, as a distinct being, he can relate to them fully and creatively.

The Hero throws the boy up against the limits, against the seemingly intractable. It encourages him to dream the impossible dream that might just be possible after all, if he has enough courage. It empowers him to fight the unbeatable foe that, if he is not *possessed* by the Hero, he might just be able to defeat.

Once again, it is our position that all too often therapists, not to mention relatives, friends, co-workers, and people in positions of authority, attack, knowingly or unknowingly, the "shining" of the Hero in men. Ours is not an age that wants heroes. Ours is an age of envy, in which laziness and self-involvement are the rule. Anyone who tries to shine, who dares to stand above the crowd, is dragged back down by his lackluster and self-appointed "peers."

We need a great rebirth of the heroic in our world. Every sector of human society, wherever that may be on the planet, seems to be slipping into an unconscious chaos. Only the heroic consciousness, exerting all its might, will be able to stop this slide toward oblivion. Only a massive rebirth of courage in both men and women will rescue the world. Against enormous odds, the Hero picks up his sword and charges into the heart of the abyss, into the mouth of the dragon, into the castle under the power of an evil spell.

What is the end of the Hero? Almost universally, in legend and myth, he "dies," is transformed into a god, and translated into Heaven. We recall the story of Jesus' resurrection and ascension, or of Oedipus's final disappearance in a flash of light at Colonus, or Elijah's ascent into the sky in a fiery chariot.

The "death" of the Hero is the "death" of boyhood, of Boy psychology. And it is the birth of manhood and Man psychology. The "death" of the Hero in the life of a boy (or a man) really means that he has finally encountered his limitations. He has met the enemy, and the enemy is himself. He has met his own dark side, his very *un*heroic side. He has fought the dragon and been burned by it; he has fought the revolution and drunk the dregs of his own inhumanity. He has overcome the Mother and then realized his incapacity to love the Princess. The "death" of the Hero signals a boy's or man's encounter with true humility. It is the end of his heroic consciousness.

True humility, we believe, consists of two things. The first is knowing our limitations. And the second is getting the help we need.

If we are possessed by the Hero, we will fall under the negative aspect of this energy and live out—as Tom Cruise's character did—the inflated feelings and actions of the Grandstander Bully. We will walk over others in our insensitivity and arrogance, and eventually we will self-destruct, ridiculed and cast out by others. If we are in the passive pole of the Hero's bipolar Shadow, possessed by the Coward, we will lack the motivation to achieve anything of significance for human life. But if we access the Hero energy appropriately, we will push ourselves up against our limitations. We will adventure to the frontiers of what we can be as boys, and from there, if we can make the transition, we will be prepared for our initiation into manhood.

4.   *Man Psychology*

It is enormously difficult for a human being to develop to full potential. The struggle with the infantile within us exerts a tremendous "gravitational" pull against achieving that full adult potential. Nevertheless, we need to fight gravity by dint of hard labor and to build the pyramids of first boyhood and then manhood that constitute the core structures of our masculine Selves. The ancient Maya seldom destroyed earlier structures from their cities' pasts. Like them, we do not want to demolish the pyramids of boyhood, for they were and will always remain generators of power and gateways to energy resources from our primordial past. But we need to get to work laying courses of stone over those old terraces and stairs. We need to build, brick by brick, toward the goal of mature masculinity, until at last we can stand on the high platform at the top, surveying our realm as "Lord of the Four Quarters."

There are a number of techniques we can use in this construction project. Analysis of dreams, the re-entering and changing of our dreams, active imagination (in which the Ego, among other things, dialogues with the energy patterns within, thereby achieving both differentiation from and access to them), psychotherapy in a variety of forms, meditation on the positive aspects of the archetypes, prayer, magical ritual process with a spiritual elder, various forms of spiritual discipline, and other methods are all important to the difficult process of turning boys into men.

The four major forms of the mature masculine energies that we have identified are the King, the Warrior, the Magician, and the Lover. They all overlap and, ideally, enrich one another. A good King is always also a Warrior, a Magician, and a Lover. And the same holds true for the other three.

The boy energies also overlap and inform each other, as we've seen. The Divine Child naturally gives rise to the Oedipal Child. Together they form the nucleus of whatever will be beautiful, energetic, related, warm, caring, and spiritual in the man. The boy's Ego needs the Precocious Child's perceptiveness to help it to distinguish itself from these energies. And all three give rise to the Hero, which breaks them free of the domination of the "feminine" unconscious, and establishes the boy's identity as a separate individual. The Hero prepares the boy to become a man.

The archetypes are mysterious entities or energy flows. They have been compared to a magnet beneath a sheet of paper. As iron filings are sprinkled over the top of the paper, they immediately arrange themselves into patterns along the lines of magnetic force. We can see the patterns of the filings on the paper, but we can't see the magnet beneath the paper—or, better, we can never see the magnetic force itself, only the visible evidence of its existence. The same is true of archetypes. They remain hidden. But we experience their effects—in art, in poetry, in music, in religion, in our scientific discoveries, in our patterns of behavior and of thought and feeling. All the products of human creativity and human interaction are like the iron filings. We can see something of the shapes and patterns of the archetypes through these manifestations. But we can never see the "energies" themselves. They overlap and interpenetrate one another, yet they can be distinguished from one another for purposes of clarification. Through active imagination, they can be remixed so that we can realize the desired balance among their influences in our own lives.

Jean Shinoda Bolen has usefully suggested that we think of this process, untangling and isolating the archetypes and then remixing them and blending them, as a well-run board meeting. Here, the chair asks each of the officers to speak his or her mind honestly and openly about the question at hand. A good chair always wants the full input, with reasons why, from each of the people that make up the board. Some opinions will be unpopular, some, seemingly, downright dumb. Some board members may habitually seem depreciating and destructive;

others may frequently come up with brilliant ideas. It is the advice of the latter that is usually followed, though sometimes the words of truth are really spoken by the disgruntled and negative board members. But after all opinions have been heard and the matter has been thoroughly discussed, the chair calls for a vote, and the decision is made. Often the chair must cast the deciding vote.

Our Egos are like the chair of the board. And the board members are the archetypes within us. Each needs to be heard from. Each needs to stand on its own and provide its input. But the whole person under the supervision of the Ego needs to make the final decisions in our lives.

Man psychology, as we have suggested, has perhaps always been a rare thing on our planet. It is certainly a rare thing today. The horrible physical and psychological circumstances under which most human beings have lived most places, most of the time, are staggering. Hostile environments always lead to the stunting, twisting, and mutating of an organism. *Why* this should be so is the stuff of which philosophy and theology are made. Let us frankly admit the enormous difficulty of our situation, for it is only when we allow ourselves to see the seriousness of any problem and to admit what it is we are up against that we can begin to take appropriate action, action that will be life-enhancing for us and for others.

There's a saying in psychology that we have to take responsibility for what we're not responsible for. This means that we are not responsible (as no infant is) for what happened to us to stunt us and to fixate us in our early years when our personalities were formed and when we got stuck at immature levels of masculinity. Yet it does us no good to join the chorus of the delinquents in *West Side Story* as they plead their case against society and leave things at that.

Ours is a psychological age rather than an institutional one. What used to be done for us by institutional structures and through ritual process, we now have to do inside ourselves, for ourselves. Ours is a culture of the individual rather than the collective.

Our Western civilization pushes us to strike out on our own, to become, as Jung said, "individuated" from each other. That which used to be more or less unconsciously shared by everyone—like the process of developing a mature masculine identity—we now must connect with consciously and individually. It is to this task that we now turn.

Jan. 21   Sep. 19   March 21   8 – 19
May 21   June 21   8 – 4
                                  7 - 4

PART II

*Decoding the Male Psyche—
The Four Archetypes
of the Mature Masculine*

5.   *The KING*

The King energy is primal in all men. It bears the same relationship to the other three mature masculine potentials as the Divine Child does to the other three immature masculine energies. It comes first in importance, and it underlies and includes the rest of the archetypes in perfect balance. The good and generative King is also a good Warrior, a positive Magician, and a great Lover. And yet, with most of us, the King comes on line last. We could say that the King is the Divine Child, but seasoned and complex, wise, and in a sense as self*less* as the Divine Child is cosmically *self-involved*. The good King is wise with "the wisdom of Solomon."

Whereas the Divine Child, especially in his aspect as the High Chair Tyrant, has infantile pretensions to Godhood, the King archetype comes close to being God in his masculine form within every man. It is the primordial man, the Adam, what the philosophers call the Anthropos in each of us. Hindus call this primal masculinity in men the Atman; Jews and Christians speak of it as the *imago Dei*, the "Image of God." Freud talked about the King as the "primal father of the primal horde." And in many ways the King energy is Father energy. It is our experience, however, that although the King underlies the Father archetype, it is more extensive and more basic than the Father.

Historically, kings have always been sacred. As mortal men, however, they have been relatively unimportant. It is the kingship, or the King energy itself, that has been important. We all know the famous cry when a king dies and another is waiting to ascend the throne, "The king is dead; long live the king!" The mortal man who incarnates the King energy or bears it for a while in the service of his fellow human beings, in the service of the realm (of whatever dimensions), in the service of the cosmos, is almost an interchangeable part, a human vehicle for bringing this ordering and generative archetype into the world and into the lives of human beings.

As Sir James Frazer and others have observed, kings in the ancient world were often ritually killed when their ability to live out the King archetype began to fail. What was important was that the generative power of the energy not be tied to the fate of an aging and increasingly impotent mortal. With the raising up of the new king, the King energy was reembodied, and the King as archetype was renewed in the lives of the people of the realm. In fact, the whole world was renewed.

This pattern—this ritual killing and reviving—is what lies behind the Christian story of the death and resurrection of Christ, the Savior King. The danger for men who become *possessed* by this energy is that they too will fulfill the ancient pattern and die prematurely.

In chapter 3, we said that the "death" of the archetypes of boyhood, and especially the Hero, was the birth of the man, that the end of Boy psychology is the beginning of Man psychology. What, then, happens when the Hero—the adolescent boy—is "killed"?

The dream of one young man, right on the cusp of his making the transition from boyhood to manhood, illustrates this moment of the Hero's death and shows what form, eventually, his new masculine maturity might take. It shows the coming on line of the King energy— not to be fully realized for years to come. Here's the dream:

> I am a soldier of fortune in ancient China. I've been creating a lot of trouble, hurting a lot of people, disturbing the order of the empire for my own profit and benefit. I'm a kind of outlaw, a kind of mercenary.
>
> I'm being chased through the countryside, through a forest, by soldiers of the Chinese army, the Chinese emperor's men. We're all dressed in some kind of scale armor, with bows and arrows and probably swords. I'm running through the woods, and I see a hole in the ground, the entrance to a cave, so I rush into it to hide. Once inside, I see that it is a long tunnel. I run along the tunnel. The Chinese army sees me go into the cave, and they run after me down the tunnel.

At the end of the tunnel, I see in the far distance a pale blue light streaming down from above, from what is probably an opening in the rock. As I get closer, I see that the light is falling into a chamber, an underground chamber, and that in the chamber is a very green garden. And standing in the middle of the garden is the Chinese emperor himself in his elaborate red and gold robes. There is nowhere for me to go. The army is closing on me from behind. I am forced into the presence of the emperor himself.

There is nothing to do but to kneel before him, to submit to him. I feel great humility, as though a phase of my life is over. He looks down at me with a fatherly compassion. He's not angry with me at all. I feel from him that he has seen it all, that he has lived it all, all the adventures of life—poverty, wealth, women, wars, palace intrigues, betrayals and being betrayed, suffering and joy, everything in human life. It is out of this seasoned, very ancient, very experienced wisdom that he now treats me with compassion.

He says very gently, "You have to die. You will be executed in three hours." I know that he is right. There is a bond between us. It's as though he's been in exactly my position before; he knows about these things. With a great feeling of peace, and even happiness, I submit to my fate.

In this dream we see the heroic Boy Ego of the soldier of fortune finally meeting his limits, meeting his necessary fate, in the presence of the King. What happens to the boy is that he comes into right relationship with the primal King within and is reconciled with the "Father," as Joseph Campbell puts it.

John W. Perry, the well-known psychotherapist, discovered the King's power to heal by reorganizing the personality in the dreams and visions of schizophrenic patients. In psychotic episodes, and in other liminal states of mind, images of the sacred King would rush up from the depths of his patients' unconscious. In his book about this, *Roots of Renewal in Myth and Madness,* he describes a young male patient who kept drawing pictures of Greek columns and then associated them with a figure he called "the white king." Other case reports tell of a patient's seeing the "Queen of the Sea," and a great wedding between the patient as Queen of the Sea with the Great King, or of the pope suddenly intervening to save the visioner.

Perry realized that what his patients were describing were images that exactly paralleled the images found in ancient myths and rituals about the sacred kings. And he saw that, to the extent that his clients got in touch with these King energies, they got better. There was something about the King—in ancient times and in the dreams and visions of his suffering patients—that was immensely organizing, ordering, and creatively healing. He saw in their visions the ancient mythic battles of the great kings against the forces of chaos and the attacks of the demons, and then the glorious enthronement of the victorious kings at the center of the world. Perry realized that the King is, in fact, what he calls "the central archetype," around which the rest of the psyche is organized. He saw that it was at those moments in which his patients had "lowered levels of consciousness," when the barriers were down between their conscious identities and the powerful world of the unconscious, that creative, generative, and life-enhancing images of the King arose. People moved from craziness to greater health.

What happened with Perry's patients is parallel to what happened in the young man's dream of the Chinese emperor. The infantile Ego let go, fell into the unconscious, and met up with the King. Boy psychology vanished as Man psychology came on line and reorganized and restructured the personality.

The Two Functions of the King in His Fullness

Two functions of King energy make this transition from Boy psychology to Man psychology possible. The first of these is ordering; the second is the providing of fertility and blessing.

The King, as Perry says, is the "central archetype." Like the Divine Child, the good King is at the Center of the World. He sits on his throne on the central mountain, or on the Primeval Hill, as the ancient Egyptians called it. And from this central place, all of creation radiates in geometrical form out to the very frontiers of the realm. "World" is defined as that part of reality that is organized and ordered by the King. What is outside the boundaries of his influence is noncreation, chaos, the demonic, and nonworld.

This function of the King energy shows up everywhere in ancient mythology and in ancient interpretations of actual history. In ancient Egyptian mythology, as James Breasted and Henri Frankfort have shown, the world arose from the formlessness and chaos of a vast ocean in the form of a central Hill, or Mound. It came into being by the decree, by the sacred "Word," of the Father god, Ptah, god of wisdom and order. Yahweh, in the Bible, creates in exactly the same way. Words, in fact, define our reality; they define our worlds. We organize our lives and our worlds by concepts, by our thoughts about them, and we can only think in terms of words. In this sense, at least, words make our reality and make our universe real.

The Primeval Hill spread as land was created, and from that central ordering, then, arose all life, the gods and goddesses, human beings, and all of their cultural achievements. And with the coming of the pharaohs, the successors of the gods, the world, defined by the sacred kings, spread out in all directions from the pharaohs' throne on the Primeval Hill. This was the account the Egyptians gave of the birth of their civilization.

In ancient Mesopotamia, one of the great founding kings of that civilization, Sargon of Akkad, carved out a kingdom, built a civilization, and called himself "He Who Rules the Four Quarters." In ancient thought, not only does the world radiate from a center, but it is geometrically organized into four quarters. It is a circle divided by a cross. The Egyptian pyramids—themselves images of the central Mound—were oriented toward the four compass points, toward "the four quarters." Ancient maps were drawn schematically with this idea. And all of the ancient Mediterranean, as well as Chinese and other Asian civilizations, had the same view. Even in the perspective of the Native Americans, who presumably had no contact with the other continents and other civilizations, this was so. The Sioux medicine man Black Elk in John Neihardt's book *Black Elk Speaks* talks about the world as a great "hoop," divided by two paths, a "red path" and a "black path," which intersect. Where they intersect is the central mountain of the world. It is on that mountain that the great Father God—the King energy—speaks and gives Black Elk a series of revelations for his people.

Ancient peoples located the Center in many places: Mount Sinai, Jerusalem, Hierapolis, Olympus, Rome, Tenochtitlán. But it was always the Center of a quadrated universe, an orderly, geometrical universe. The Center of that universe was always where the king—god and man—reigned, and was the locus of divine revelation, of divine organizing and creative power.

What is really interesting for us about this view of the ordering function of the King energy is that it shows up not only in ancient maps, in the sand paintings of desert Indians, in the icons of Buddhist art, and in the rose windows of Christian churches, but also just as persistently in the dreams and paintings of modern people undergoing psychoanalysis. Jung, noticing this, borrowed the name for such representations from Tibetan Buddhism and called these pictures of the organizing Center "mandalas." He noticed that when mandalas appeared in his analysands' dreams and visions, they were always healing and life-giving. They always signified renewal, and, like Perry's images of the King, they showed that the personality was reorganizing in a more centered way, becoming more structured and calmer.

What this function of the King energy does, through a mortal king, is embody for the people of the realm this ordering principle of the Divine World. The human king does this by codifying laws. He makes laws, or more accurately, he receives them from the King energy itself and then passes them on to his nation.

In the Oriental Institute Museum in Chicago there is a full-size reproduction of the great pillar of laws of the ancient Babylonian king Hammurabi (1728–1686 B.C.E.). The "pillar" is actually in the shape of a giant forefinger pointing upward, saying, in effect, "Listen! This is it! This is how things are going to be!" And where the fingernail is on this giant finger is a picture of Hammurabi standing in contemplation, scratching his long beard, listening to the great Father god Shamash— the sun, king of the gods—the supreme symbol of the light of masculine consciousness. Shamash is giving Hammurabi the laws that are inscribed below and all around the sides of the finger. The finger itself is what the ancients called, when referring to the will of God, "the finger of God." The picture of Hammurabi receiving the laws is expressing the primordial or archetypal incident—ever recurring—of the King energy

Shah Nameh (From a seventeenth-century Indian illuminated manuscript. Courtesy of Musée Condé, Chantilly, France. Photo: Giraudon/Art Resource.)

giving his human servant, the mortal king, the key to peace, calm, and order. This same timeless event is depicted in the biblical story of Moses receiving the Torah from Yahweh on the primordial mountain, Sinai.

This mysterious order, expressed in the kingdom and even in its palaces and temples (often laid out as representations of the cosmos in miniature) and in human laws and in all human societal order—customs, traditions, and spoken and unspoken taboos—is the manifestation of the ordering thoughts of the Creator God. In Ancient Egyptian mythology, this was alternately thought of as the god Ptah or as a goddess called Ma'at, "Right Order." We see this idea carried forward in early Hebrew thought in the figure of Wisdom in the biblical book of Proverbs, and even in the Greek and later Christian idea of Christ as the Logos, the ordering, generative, and creative Word the Gospel of John talks about. In Hinduism, this archetypal "right order" is called Dharma. In China, it is called the Tao, the "Way."

It is the mortal king's duty not only to receive and take to his people this right order of the universe and cast it in societal form but, even more fundamentally, to embody it in his own person, to live it in his own life. The mortal king's first responsibility is to live according to Ma'at, or Dharma, or the Tao. If he does, the mythology goes, everything in the kingdom—that is, the creation, the world—will also go according to the Right Order. The kingdom will flourish. If the king does not live "in the Tao" then nothing will go right for his people, or for the kingdom as a whole. The realm will languish, the Center, which the king represents, will not hold, and the kingdom will be ripe for rebellion.

When this happened in the Middle Kingdom of ancient Egyptian history, we find the prophet Nefer-rohu describing the disastrous social and economic consequences to Egypt of the rule of illegitimate kings, kings who did not live according to Ma'at. (We recall the blight on the land of Thebes that accompanied Oedipus's impious reign.) Nefer-rohu writes:

> Re [another form of the Creator God] must begin the foundation [of the earth over again]. The land is completely perished. . . . The sun disc is covered over. . . . It will not shine. . . . The rivers of Egypt are empty. . . .

Damaged indeed are those good things, those fish-ponds, [where there were] those who clean fish, overflowing with fish and fowl. Everything good is disappeared. . . . Foes have arisen in the east, and Asiatics have come down into Egypt. . . . The wild beasts of the desert will drink at the rivers of Egypt. . . . This land is helter-skelter. . . . Men will take up weapons of warfare, [so that] the land lives in confusion. Men will make arrows of metal, beg for the bread of blood, and laugh with the laughter of sickness. . . . [A] man's heart pursues himself [alone]. . . . A man sits in his corner, [turning] his back while one kills another. I show thee a son as a foe, the brother as an enemy, and a man killing his [own] father.

Then Nefer-rohu prophesies that a new king will arise who embodies the principles of Right Order. This king will restore Egypt, and set the cosmos aright:

[Then] it is that a king will come, belonging to the south, Ameni, the triumphant, his name. He is the son of a woman of the land of Nubia; he is one born in Upper Egypt. He will take the [White] Crown; he will wear the Red Crown; he will unite the Two Mighty Ones; he will satisfy the Two Lords with what they desire. The encircler-of-the-fields [will be] in his grasp. . . . Rejoice, ye people of his time! The son of a man will make his name forever and ever. They who incline toward evil and who plot rebellion have subdued their speech for fear of him. The Asiatics will fall to his sword, and the Libyans will fall to his flame. . . . There will be built the Wall of the Ruler of life, prosperity, health!—and the Asiatics will not be permitted to come down into Egypt. . . . And justice will come into its place, while wrongdoing is driven out. Rejoice, he who may behold [this]!*

In the same way, the Chinese emperors ruled by the "Mandate of Heaven." Heaven here means, again, "right order." And when they failed to live according to the will of Heaven, then, legitimately, there would be rebellion, and a new dynasty would be established. "The king is dead; long live the king!"

First, the mortal king, operating under the mature masculine energy of the King, lived the order in his own life; only secondarily did

---

* Quoted in James B. Pritchard, ed., *The Ancient Near East: An Anthology of Texts and Pictures* (Princeton: Princeton Univ. Press, 1958), pp. 254–257.

he enforce it. And he did so both in his realm and on the outskirts of the kingdom at the point of interface between the creation and the outlying chaos. Here we see the King as the Warrior, extending and defending order against the "Asiatics" and the "Libyans."

The mortal king did this historically as the servant and earthly embodiment of the King archetype, which maintained order in the spiritual world, or the deep and timeless world of the unconscious. Here we see the stories of the Babylonian god Marduk fighting the forces of chaos in the form of the dragon Tiamat and beating her demon army, slaying her, and creating the ordered world from her body. Or we see the Canaanite Baal slaying the twin monsters of chaos and death, Yamm and Mot. We also see this function of the King energy in the so-called enthronement psalms in the Bible, in which Yahweh (the Hebrew God Jehovah) defeats the dragon Behemoth, or Tehom, and then ascends his throne to order and create the world.

On a more immediate note, we see in modern dysfunctional families that when there is an immature, a weak, or an absent father and the King energy is not sufficiently present, the family is very often given over to disorder and chaos.

In conjunction with his ordering function, the second vital good that the King energy manifests is fertility and blessing. Ancient peoples always associated fertility—in human beings, crops, herds, and the natural world in general—with the creative ordering of things by the gods. It seems that in prepatriarchal times, the earth as Mother was seen as the primary source of fertility. But as patriarchal cultures rose to ascendancy, the emphasis shifted from the feminine as the source of fertility to the masculine. This was not a simple shift, and the emphasis never shifted completely. The ancient myths, true to actual biology, recognized that it was the union of male and female that was truly generative, at least on the physical plane. On the cultural plane, however, in the creation of civilization and technology, and in the mastery of the natural world, the masculine generative energies were most prominent.

The sacred king in ancient times became the primary expression for many peoples of the life-force, the libido, of the cosmos. Our Jewish, Christian, and Moslem God today is never seen as being in creative partnership with a Goddess. He is viewed as male, and as the sole source of creativity and generativity. He is the sole source of fertility and blessing. Many of our modern beliefs come from the beliefs of the ancient patriarchies.

The sacred king's function of providing fertility and blessing shows up in many myths and in the stories of great kings. In the spiritual world, we see the great Father gods engaging prolifically in sexual relationships with goddesses, lesser deities, and mortal women. The Egyptian Amun-Ra had his harem in the sky, and Zeus's exploits are well known.

But it was not just sexual acts producing both divine and human children that showed the King energy's capacity to fertilize. This capacity to be generative was also the result of his creative ordering itself. The Canaanite Baal, for instance, after he defeated the dragon of the chaotic sea, and because he loved the earth, ordered the chaotic waters into rainfall and rivers and streams. This ordering act made it possible for the first time for plants to flourish, and then animals. And it made the bounty of agriculture and herding possible for human beings, his special beneficiaries.

In the Egyptian "Hymn to Aton" (the Sun), it was Aton who ordered the world so that it could prosper and be fertile. He put the Nile in Egypt so that birds could rise from their nests in the reeds, singing joyfully for the life Aton had given them, so that herds could grow and calves could flick their tails in happiness and contentment. Aton put a "Nile in the sky" for other peoples, so that they too could experience the abundance of life. And Aton so ordered the world that every race and every tongue would have the blessing of life and fecundity, each in its own way, according to Aton's design.

As the mortal king went, so did the realm, both its order and fertility. If the king was lusty and vigorous sexually, could service his often many wives and concubines and produce many children, the land would be vital. If he stayed healthy and strong physically, and alert and alive mentally, the crops would grow; the cattle would reproduce; the merchants would prosper; and many babies would be born to his people. The rains would come and, in Egypt, the annual fertilizing Nile floods.

In the Bible, we see the same idea expressed in the stories of the Hebrew kings and patriarchs. Two things were required of them by

Yahweh: first, that they walk in his ways, the Hebrew equivalent of being in the Tao; and second, that they "be fruitful and multiply," that they have many wives and many children. We see with the patriarchs Abraham, Isaac, and Jacob that if one wife could not produce children, she would find another wife or a concubine for her husband so that he could continue his fertility function.

We see King David taking many a woman of his realm, and having children through her. The point is that as these men prospered physically and psychologically, so did their tribes and their realms. The mortal king, so goes the mythology, was the embodiment of the King energy. The land, his kingdom, was the embodiment of the feminine energies. He was, in fact, symbolically wedded to the land.

Always, the king's culminating ordering/generative act was to marry the land in the form of his primary queen. It was only in creative partnership with her that he could assure every kind of bounty for his kingdom. It was the royal couple's duty to pass their creative energies on to the kingdom in the form of children. The kingdom would mirror the royal generativity, which, let us remember, was at the Center. As the Center was, so would be the rest of creation.

When a king became sick or weak or impotent, the kingdom languished. The rains did not come. The crops did not grow. The cattle did not reproduce. The merchants lost their trade. Drought would assault the land, and the people would perish.

So the king was the earthly conduit from the Divine World—the world of the King energy—to this world. He was the mediator between the mortal and the divine, like Hammurabi standing before Shamash. He was the central artery, we might say, that allowed the blood of the life-force to flow into the human world. Because he was at the Center, in a certain sense everything in the kingdom (because it owed its existence to him) was his—all the crops, all the cattle, all the people, all the women. That was in theory, however. The mortal king David ran afoul of this principle in his liaison with the beautiful Bathsheba. But this moves us into the discussion of the Shadow King, which we'll turn to in a moment.

It was not only fertility in an immediately physical sense or generativity and creativity in a general sense that came out of the second function of the King energy through the efficacy of ancient kings; it was also blessing. Blessing is a psychological, or spiritual, event. The good king always mirrored and affirmed others who deserved it. He did this by seeing them—in a literal sense, in his audiences at the palace, and in the psychological sense of noticing them, knowing them, in their true worth. The good king delighted in noticing and promoting good men to positions of responsibility in his kingdom. He held audience, primarily, not to be seen (although this was important to the extent that he carried the people's own projected inner King energy), but to see, admire, and delight in his subjects, to reward them and to bestow honors upon them.

There is a beautiful ancient Egyptian painting of the Pharaoh Akhenaton standing in his royal balcony, splendidly embraced by the rays of his Father god, Aton, the sun, throwing rings of gold down to his best followers, his most competent and loyal men. By the light of the masculine sun-consciousness, he knows his men. He recognizes them, and he is generative toward them. He bestows upon them his blessing. Being blessed has tremendous psychological consequences for us. There are even studies that show that our bodies actually change chemically when we feel valued, praised, and blessed.

Young men today are starving for blessing from older men, starving for blessing from the King energy. This is why they cannot, as we say, "get it together." They shouldn't have to. They need to be blessed. They need to be seen by the King, because if they are, something inside will come together for them. That is the effect of blessing; it heals and makes whole. That's what happens when we are seen and valued and concretely rewarded (with gold, perhaps, dropped from the pharaoh's hand) for our legitimate talents and abilities.

Of course, many ancient kings, like many men in "kingly" positions today, fell far short of the ideal image of the good King. Yet this central archetype lives on independently of any one of us and seeks, through us, to come into our lives in order to consolidate, create, and bless.

What can we say are the characteristics of the good King? Based on ancient myths and legends, what are the qualities of this mature masculine energy?

The King archetype in its fullness possesses the qualities of order, of reasonable and rational patterning, of integration and integrity in the masculine psyche. It stabilizes chaotic emotion and out-of-control behaviors. It gives stability and centeredness. It brings calm. And in its "fertilizing" and centeredness, it mediates vitality, life-force, and joy. It brings maintenance and balance. It defends our own sense of inner order, our own integrity of being and of purpose, our own central calmness about who we are, and our essential unassailability and certainty in our masculine identity. It looks upon the world with a firm but kindly eye. It sees others in all their weakness and in all their talent and worth. It honors them and promotes them. It guides them and nurtures them toward their own fullness of being. It is not envious, because it is secure, as the King, in its own worth. It rewards and encourages creativity in us and in others.

In its central incorporation and expression of the Warrior, it represents aggressive might when that is what is needed when order is threatened. It also has the power of inner authority. It knows and discerns (its Magician aspect) and acts out of this deep knowingness. It delights in us and in others (its Lover aspect) and shows this delight through words of authentic praise and concrete actions that enhance our lives.

This is the energy that expresses itself through a man when he takes the necessary financial and psychological steps to ensure that his wife and children prosper. This is the energy that encourages his wife when she decides she wants to go back to school to become a lawyer. This is the energy that expresses itself through a father when he takes time off from work to attend his son's piano recital. This is the energy that, through the boss, confronts the rebellious subordinates at the office without firing them. This is the energy that expresses itself through the assembly line foreman when he is able to work with the recovering alcoholics and drug abusers in his charge to support their sobriety and to give them empowering masculine guidance and nurturing.

This is the energy that expresses itself through you when you are able to keep your cool when everybody else in the meeting is losing theirs. This is the voice of calm and reassurance, the encouraging word in a time of chaos and struggle. This is the clear decision, after careful deliberation, that cuts through the mess in the family, at work, in the nation, in the world. This is the energy that seeks peace and stability, orderly growth and nurturing for all people—and not only for all people, but for the environment, the natural world. The King cares for the whole realm and is the steward of nature as well as of human society.

This is the energy, manifested in ancient myths, of the "shepherd of his people" and "the gardener" and husbandman of the plants and animals in the kingdom. This is the voice that affirms, clearly and calmly and with authority, the human rights of all. This is the energy that minimizes punishment and maximizes praise. This is the voice from the Center, the Primeval Hill within every man.

The Shadow King: The Tyrant and the Weakling

Though most of us have experienced some of this energy of the mature masculine in our lives—perhaps within ourselves in moments when we felt very well integrated, calm, and centered, and from time to time from our father, a kindly uncle or grandfather, a co-worker, a boss, a teacher, a minister—most of us also have to confess that overall we have experienced very little of the King energy in its fullness. We may have felt it in bits and pieces, but the sad fact is that this positive energy is disastrously lacking in the lives of most men. Mostly what we have experienced is what we are calling the Shadow King.

As in the case of all of the archetypes, the King displays an active-passive bipolar shadow structure. We call the active pole of the Shadow King the Tyrant and the passive pole the Weakling.

We can see the Tyrant acting in the Christian story of the birth of Jesus. Soon after the Christ child is born, King Herod discovers the fact that the infant has been born and is in the world, the world that he, King Herod, controls. He sends his soldiers to Bethlehem looking for the new king—the new life—to kill it. Because Jesus is a Divine Child, he gets away in time. But Herod's soldiers kill every male child left in the town. Whenever the new is born, the Herod within us (and in our outer lives) will attack. The tyrant hates, fears, and envies new life, because that new life, he senses, is a threat to his slim grasp on his own kingship. The tyrant king is not in the Center and does not feel calm and generative. He is not creative, only destructive. If he were secure in his own generativity and in his own inner order—his Self structures—he would react with delight at the birth of new life in his realm. If Herod had been such a man, he would have realized that the time had come for him to step aside so that the archetype could be embodied in the new king Jesus Christ.

Another biblical story, the story of Saul, has a similar theme. Saul is another mortal king who became possessed by the Tyrant. His reaction to the newly anointed David is the same as Herod's to Jesus. He reacts with fear and rage and seeks to kill David. Though the prophet Samuel has told Saul that Yahweh no longer wants him to be king—that is, to embody the King energy for the realm—Saul's Ego has become identified with the King and refuses to relinquish the throne. Human tyrants are those in kingly positions (whether in the home, the office, the White House, or the Kremlin) who are identified with the King energy and fail to realize that they are not it.

Another example, from antiquity, is that of the Roman emperor Caligula. Although the previous emperors had held enormous power over the people and the Senate of Rome and, through their office, over the entire Mediterranean world, and although they had been turned into gods after their deaths, Caligula broke new ground when he declared himself a god while still on earth. The details of his madness and of his abuse and sadism toward all those around him are fascinating. Robert Graves's book *I, Claudius* and the television series based on the book give a chilling account of the development of the Shadow King as Tyrant in the person of Caligula.

The Tyrant exploits and abuses others. He is ruthless, merciless, and without feeling when he is pursuing what he thinks is his own self-interest. His degradation of others knows no bounds. He hates all beauty, all innocence, all strength, all talent, all life energy. He does so because, as we've said, he lacks inner structure, and he is afraid—terrified, really—of his own hidden weakness and his underlying lack of potency.

It is the Shadow King as Tyrant in the father who makes war on his sons' (and his daughters') joy and strength, their abilities and vitality. He fears their freshness, their newness of being, and the life-force surging through them, and he seeks to kill it. He does this with open verbal assaults and deprecation of their interests, hopes, and talents; or he does it, alternately, by ignoring their accomplishments, turning his

King Arthur (Illustration by Trevor Stubley from *The Book of Merlyn* by T. H. White, © 1977. Reproduced by permission of the University of Texas Press, Austin.)

back on their disappointments, and registering boredom and lack of interest when, for instance, they come home from school and present him with a piece of artwork or a good grade on a test.

His attacks may not be limited to verbal or psychological abuse; they may include physical abuse. Spankings may turn into beatings. And there may be sexual assaults as well. The father possessed by the Tyrant may sexually exploit his daughters' or even his sons' weakness and vulnerability.

A young woman came for counseling because she was having a lot of trouble in her marriage. What she described, soon after entering therapy, was an invasion of her home by the Tyrant King in this sexually malignant aspect. At about the age of twelve, her father had left her, her mother, and her sister and moved in with another woman. That woman's husband had then moved in with them. This man never liked his new "wife," and he was quick to spot his new stepdaughter's beauty and vulnerability. He began demanding that she sleep with him, at first just lying beside him in bed at night. Then he began demanding that she masturbate him, so that he ejaculated into tissues that he kept by the bed. Eventually, he forced her to have sex with him, on the threat that if she didn't, he would leave them, and they would have nowhere to turn financially. The young woman's mother never made a move to stop this horrendous abuse of her daughter and busied herself in the mornings cleaning under the mattress where the soiled tissues from the night before had been stuffed.

In the story of King David and Bathsheba, Bathsheba was the wife of another man, Uriah the Hittite. One day David was walking on the roof of his palace when he spotted Bathsheba bathing. He was so aroused by this sight that he sent for her and forced her to have sex with him. In theory, remember, all the women of the realm were the king's. But they belonged to the *archetype* of the King, not to the mortal king. David unconsciously identified himself with the King energy and not only took Bathsheba but also had her husband, Uriah, killed. Fortunately for the kingdom, David had a conscience in the form of Nathan the prophet, who came to him and indicted him. David, much to his credit, accepted the truth of the indictment and repented.

The Tyrant King manifests in all of us at some time or another when we feel pushed to the limit, when we are exhausted, when we are getting inflated. But we can see it operating most of the time in certain personality configurations, most notably in the so-called narcissistic personality disorder. These people really feel that they are the center of the universe (although they aren't centered themselves) and that others exist to serve them. Instead of mirroring *others*, they insatiably seek mirroring *from* them. Instead of seeing others, they seek to be seen by them.

We can also observe the Tyrant King operating in certain ways of life, even in certain "professions." The drug lords, the pimps, the mafia bosses are all examples; they exist to further their own status, and what they think is their own well-being, at the expense of others. But we see this same self-interest in societally sanctioned positions as well. An interviewer should enter into a dialogue with you about your experience, your training, your hopes for yourself and the company you are seeking to serve. Instead, he spends the whole interview talking about *himself* and *his* achievements, *his* power, *his* salary, and the virtues of *his* company, and never asks you about yourself.

Many people in corporate America today are not at all interested in the companies they work for. Many are just "treading water," looking for a way out and up. Here we find the executives who are more interested in furthering their own careers than in being good stewards of the "realms" placed under their authority. There is no devotion or real loyalty to the company, only to themselves. This is the CEO who negotiates, for his own financial benefit, to sell his company, to see it dismembered and rendered impotent, who is willing to see his friends and loyal employees fired as excess baggage in the now popular "leveraged buy-out."

The man possessed by the Tyrant is very sensitive to criticism and, though putting on a threatening front, will at the slightest remark feel weak and deflated. He won't show you this, however. What you will see, unless you know what to look for, is rage. But under the rage is a sense of worthlessness, of vulnerability and weakness, for behind the Tyrant lies the other pole of the King's bipolar shadow system, the Weakling. If he can't be *identified* with the King energy, he feels he is nothing.

The hidden presence of this passive pole explains the hunger for mirroring—for "Adore me!" "Worship me!" "See how important I am!" —that we feel from so many of our superiors and friends. This explains their angry outbursts and their attacks on those they see as weak, that is, those upon whom they project their own inner Weakling. General Patton, for all his virtues, evidently had an underlying fear of his own weakness and cowardice. In the movie *Patton* this is shown when he is visiting a field hospital during World War II. He's going from bed to bed congratulating wounded men and giving them medals (something the King in his fullness does). But then he comes to the bed of a man who is suffering from "shell shock." Patton asks him what his problem is, and the soldier tells him his nerves are shot. Instead of reacting with the compassion of the life-giving King who knows what his men are up against, Patton flies into a rage and slaps the soldier across the face, calls him a coward, humiliates and abuses him, and sends him from the hospital to the front lines. Though he does not know it, what he has seen is the face of his own hidden fear and weakness projected onto another. He has glimpsed the Weakling within.

The man possessed by the Weakling lacks centeredness, calmness, and security within himself, and this also leads him into paranoia. We see this in Herod, Saul, and Caligula as all of them, unable to sleep at night, pace the palace, tormented by fears of disloyalty from their subordinates—in Saul's case, even from his children—and disapproval from God, the True King. The man possessed by the bipolar Shadow King has much to fear, *in fact*, because his oppressive behaviors, often including cruelty, beg for an in-kind response from others. We laugh at the saying, "Just because you're paranoid doesn't mean they're not out to get you." They may be. A defensive, hostile "get them before they get you" paranoia is destructive of one's own sense of calmness and order-liness, works to destroy one's own character and that of others, and invites retaliation.

A minister entered analysis a short time after a crisis had started in his church. A group of ne'er-do-well dissidents, a band of psychological and spiritual outlaws, had formed, and for their own envious reasons, they had set out to destroy this minister. The leader was a man who heard God talking to him audibly in the night and who had received a dream that told him the minister was planning to kill him for working against him. Paranoia is catching. The paranoia of the instigator of this "palace coup" so harassed this pastor day and night with phone calls, hate letters containing outright threats, outbursts in the middle of the sermons, and speeches at church meetings listing the minister's supposed failures that the minister, not consolidated in his relationship to his own King energy, gradually slipped under the power of the Tyrant/Weakling. He became increasingly tyrannical and dictatorial about church policy, arrogated more and more power to himself in church governance, and began to use shady tactics against his "enemies" in order to drive them out of the church. At the same time, he was disturbed by terrifying nightmares that, night after night, revealed to him his own underlying fears and weaknesses. Mutual paranoia raised its dark bloom, and both the minister and the congregation ended in a world of confusion and subterfuge, a world utterly removed from the spiritual values the minister had sought so lovingly to teach— another victory for the Shadow King.

We can readily see the Tyrant's relationship to the High Chair Tyrant, arising as he does out of this infantile pattern. Grandiosity is normal, in a certain way, in the Divine Child. It is appropriate for the Divine Child, like the baby Jesus, to want and need to be adored, even by kings. What parents need to do, and this is very difficult, is give the Divine Child in their own child just the right amount of adoration and affirmation, so that they can let their human child down off the "high chair" easily, gradually into the real world, where gods cannot live as mortal humans. The parents need to help their human baby boy learn gradually not to identify with the Divine Child. The boy may resist being dethroned, but the parents must persevere, both affirming him and "taking him down a peg" at a time.

If they adore him too much and don't help the baby boy's Ego form outside the archetype, then he may never get down from his high chair. Inflated with the power of the High Chair Tyrant, he will simply cross into adulthood thinking he is "Caesar." If we challenge a person like this, and say to him, "My God, you think you're Caesar!" he may very well say, "Yeah? What about it?" This is one way the Shadow King gets formed in men.

The other way the Shadow King is formed is when the parents have abused the baby boy, and attacked his grandiosity and gloriousness from the beginning. The grandiosity of the Divine Child/High Chair Tyrant then gets split off and dropped into the boy's unconscious for safekeeping. The boy may, as a consequence, come under the power of the Weakling Prince. Later, when he is an "adult" and functioning primarily under the dominance of the Weakling, under the enormous pressures of the adult world, his repressed grandiosity may explode to the surface, completely raw and primitive, completely unmodulated and very powerful. This is the man who seemed coolheaded and rational and "nice" but who, once he's been promoted, suddenly becomes "a different person," a Little Hitler. This is the man for whom the saying "Power corrupts; absolute power corrupts absolutely" is entirely accurate.

Accessing the King

The first task in accessing the King energy for would-be human "kings" is to disidentify our Egos from it. We need to achieve what psychologists call *cognitive distance* from the King in both his integrated fullness and his split bipolar shadow forms. Realistic greatness in adult life, as opposed to inflation and grandiosity, involves recognizing our proper relationship to this and the other mature masculine energies. That proper relationship is like that of a planet to the star it is orbiting. The planet is not the center of the star system; the star is. The planet's job is to keep the proper orbital distance from the life-giving, but also potentially death-dealing, star so as to enhance its own life and well-being. The planet derives its life from the star, so it has a transpersonal object in the star for "adoration." Or, to use another image, the Ego of the mature man needs to think of itself—no matter what status or power it has temporarily achieved—as the servant of a transpersonal Will, or Cause. It needs to think of itself as a steward of the King energies, not for the benefit of itself, but for the benefit of those within its "realm," whatever that may be.

There are two ways to look at the difference between the "active" and "passive" poles in the bipolar shadow system of the archetypes. As we have seen, one way is to view the archetypal structures as triangular or triune. The other way is to talk about the Ego's identification with or disidentification from the archetype in its fullness. In the case of identification, the result is Ego inflation, accompanied by fixation at infantile levels of development. In the case of extreme disidentification, the Ego experiences itself as deprived of access to the archetype. It is, in actuality, caught in the passive pole of the King's dysfunctional Shadow. The Ego feels starved for King energy. This sense of deprivation and lack of "ownership" of the sources of and motives for power are always features of the passive poles of the archetypes.

The Shadow King as Tyrant, because he arises, according to this perspective, when the Ego is identified with the King energy itself, has no transpersonal commitment. *He* is his own priority. Because a man's Ego has not been able to maintain its proper orbit, it has fallen into the sun of the archetype, or drifted so close that it has drawn off—as we see in double-star systems—enormous amounts of ignited gasses and become bloated with them. The whole psyche destabilizes. The planet pretends to be a star. The true Center of the system is lost. This is what we are calling the "usurpation syndrome." The Ego usurps the King's place and power. This is the mythological rebellion in heaven, described in so many myths, when an upstart god tries to seize the throne of the High God. (We recall the myth of Satan's attempted overthrow of God.)

The other problem in accessing this energy, we're suggesting, arises when we have lost effective touch with the life-giving King altogether (mistakenly, it turns out). In this case, we may fall into the category of the so-called dependent personality disorder, a condition in which we project the King energy within (which we do not experience as within us) onto some external person. We experience ourselves as impotent, as incapable of acting, incapable of feeling calm and stable, without the presence and the loving attention of that other person who is carrying our King energy projection. This happens in family systems when husbands become too attentive to their wives' moods and fear to take initiative because of the attacking anger their actions may bring. It happens, too, with children when their parents do not allow them to develop sufficient independence of will and taste and purpose and the children remain under their wing.

In our work situations, this happens when we become too dependent upon the power and whims of the boss, or when we feel that we don't dare sneeze around our co-workers. It also happens on the larger scale of nations, when the people, regarding themselves as peasants, turn over all their own inner King energy to "der Führer." This "abdication syndrome," the hallmark of the Weakling, is just as disastrous as the usurpation syndrome.

An example of the disastrous consequences of the abdication syndrome on a large scale is an incident that occurred on the plain of Otumba, near what is now Mexico City, during Cortés's conquest of Mexico. Cortés and his men had fled Tenochtitlán (Mexico City) in the middle of the night six days before under massive attack from the Mexican armies. As the seventh day dawned, the exhausted and fearful remains of Cortés's army looked down the plain of Otumba to see a vast host of Mexican warriors massed against them. The doom of the Spanish seemed certain. However, in the ensuing battle, Cortés spotted the banner of the Mexican commander. In desperation, knowing that their lives depended on it, Cortés charged forward, cutting a swath of carnage through the enemy soldiers. When he finally reached the Mexican commander, he killed him with one blow. Immediately, to the amazement of the Spanish, the Mexicans turned in panic and fled the field. The Spanish chased them down and slaughtered many of them. What had happened to so miraculously turn the tide of battle was that the Mexican warriors had seen their commander killed. They had invested this man with the focused power of the King energy, and when he was killed, they believed that archetypal energy had deserted them. Their underlying sense of disempowerment rose to the surface with the death of their leader, and they surrendered to impotence and chaos. If only the Mexican warriors had realized that the King energy was within them, Mexico might never have been conquered.

When we are out of touch with our own inner King and give the power over our lives to others, we may be courting catastrophe on a scale larger than the personal. Those we make our kings may lead us into lost battles, abuse in our families, mass murder, the horrors of a Nazi Germany, or a Jonestown. Or they may simply abandon us to our own underlying weakness.

But when we are accessing the King energy correctly, as servants of our own inner King, we will manifest in our own lives the qualities of the good and rightful King, the King in his fullness. Our soldiers of fortune will drop to their knees, appropriately, before the Chinese Emperor within. We will feel our anxiety level drop. We will feel centered, and calm, and hear ourselves speak from an inner authority. We will have the capacity to mirror and to bless ourselves and others. We will have the capacity to care for others deeply and genuinely. We will "recognize" others; we will behold them as the full persons they really are. We will have a sense of being a centered participant in creating a more just, calm, and creative world. We will have a transpersonal devotion not only to our families, our friends, our companies, our causes, our religions, but also to the world. We will have some kind of spirituality, and we will know the truth of the central commandment around which all of human life seems to be based: "Thou shalt love the Lord thy God [read, "the King"] with all thy heart, with all thy soul, and with all thy might. And thy neighbor as thyself."

6.   *The WARRIOR*

We live in a time when people are generally uncomfortable with the Warrior form of masculine energy—and for some good reasons. Women especially are uncomfortable with it, because they have often been the most direct victims of it in its shadow form. Around the planet, warfare in our century has reached such monstrous and pervasive proportions that aggressive energy itself is looked upon with deep suspicion and fear. This is the age in the West of the "soft masculine," and it is a time in which radical feminists raise loud and hostile voices against the Warrior energy. In the liberal churches, committees are removing such "warlike" hymns as "Onward Christian Soldiers" and "The Battle Hymn of the Republic" from the hymnals.

What is interesting to notice, however, is that those who would cut off masculine aggressiveness at its root, in their zeal, themselves fall under the power of this archetype. We can't just take a vote and vote the Warrior out. Like all archetypes, it lives on in spite of our conscious attitudes toward it. And like all *repressed* archetypes, it goes underground, eventually to resurface in the form of emotional and physical violence, like a volcano that has lain dormant for centuries with the pressure gradually building up in the magma chamber. If the Warrior is an instinctual energy form, then it is here to stay. And it pays to face it.

Jane Goodall, who lived with chimpanzee tribes for years in Africa (chimpanzees are genetically 98 percent what we are) first reported basically loving, peaceful, and good-willed animals. This report was a big hit in the sixties, when millions of people in the West were seeking to understand why warfare is such an apparently attractive human pastime to find an alternative way of settling larger-scale disputes. A few years after her initial report, however, Ms. Goodall released new evidence indicating that there was more going on than she had first thought. She discovered warfare, infanticide, child abuse, kidnaping, theft, and murder among her "peaceful" chimpanzees. Robert Ardrey, in two controversial books, *African Genesis* and *The Territorial Imperative*, claimed in the most straightforward way that human beings are governed by instincts, the same instincts that govern the feelings and behaviors of other animals—not the least of which is the urge to fight. In addition, the most current studies in the field of primate ethology suggest that the full range of human behaviors are present in our nearest primate relatives, at least in outline.

What is this phenomenon of business executives and insurance salesmen going off into the woods on the weekends to play war games, to hide among the trees and organize assaults with paint guns, to practice survival, to play at being on the edge of danger, of death, to strategize, to "kill" each other? What is the hidden energy form behind the city gangs organized along paramilitary lines? What accounts for the popularity of Rambo, of Arnold Schwarzenegger, of war movies like *Apocalypse Now, Platoon, Full-Metal Jacket*, and many, many more? We can deplore the violence in these movies, as well as on our television screens, but, obviously, the Warrior still remains very much alive within us.

All we have to do is glance over the history of our species, a history which has been *defined* in large part by war. We see the great Warrior traditions in nearly every civilization. In our century, the whole globe has been convulsed by two world wars. A third and final one, despite the recent East-West thaw, still hangs over our heads. Something is going on here. Some psychologists see human aggressiveness emerging out of infantile rage, the child's natural reaction to what Alice Miller has called "poisonous pedagogy," the abuse of baby boys (as well as baby girls) on a massive scale.

We believe there is much truth to this view, especially in light of the prevalence of what we will be calling the Shadow Warrior. But we believe that the Warrior should not be identified with human rage in any simple way—quite the opposite. We also believe that this primarily masculine energy form (there are feminine Warrior myths and traditions too) persists because the Warrior is a basic building block of masculine psychology, almost certainly rooted in our genes.

When we examine the Warrior traditions closely, we can see what they have *accomplished* in history. For example, the ancient Egyptians were for centuries a very peaceful, basically gentle people. They were safe in their isolated Nile Valley from any potential enemies; these enemies were held at bay by the surrounding desert and by the Mediterranean Sea to the north. They were able to build a remarkably stable society. They believed in the harmony of all things, in a cosmos ordered by Ma'at. Then around 1800 B.C.E. they were invaded through the Nile delta by bands of fierce Semitic tribes, the Hyksos. These Hyksos warriors had horses and chariots—in those days, efficient and devastating war machines. The Egyptians, unaccustomed to such aggressiveness, were pushovers. The Hyksos eventually took over most of Egypt and ruled it with an iron hand.

In the sixteenth century B.C.E. the hardened Egyptians eventually fought back. New pharaohs arose from the south who united their native King energy with a newfound Warrior energy. They drove northward with tremendous ferocity. Not only did they crush the Hyksos power and take Egypt back into Egyptian hands, but they continued northward into Palestine and Asia and built a vast empire. In the process, they spread Egyptian civilization—its art, religion, and ideas—over a huge area. By their conquests, the great pharaohs Thutmose III and Ramses II not only secured Egypt again, but brought the best of Egyptian culture to a larger world. It is because of their discovery of the Warrior within themselves that Egyptian morality and ethics, as well as such fundamental religious ideas as judgment after death and a paradise beyond the grave in which righteous souls would become one with God, became a part of our own Western system of ethics and spirituality. A similar story can be told about the civilizations in Mesopotamia, which also, through the energizing of the Warrior, carried important human knowledge and insights into future civilizations.

In India, a Warrior class, the *kshatriya*, conquered and stabilized the Indian subcontinent and set up the conditions for India to become the spiritual center of the world. Their cousins to the north in Persia—the Zoroastrian warrior-kings—spread the religion of Zoroaster throughout the Near East. This religion had a profound impact on the emergence of modern Judaism and Christianity and on many of the values and the basic worldview that inform and shape even our post-religious modern world. And through Western civilization, as it has come to be known, Zoroaster's teachings in modified form now sweep across the planet and affect village life and personal morality as far away as the South Seas.

The biblical Hebrews were originally a warrior people and followers of a warrior God, the God of the Hebrew scriptures, Yahweh. Under the warrior-king David, the benefits of this new religion, including its advanced ethical system based on the Warrior's virtues, were consolidated. Through Christianity, which drew heavily on its Hebrew heritage, many of these Hebrew ideas and values eventually were carried by the European warrior classes to the four corners of the world.

The Roman emperor-warriors, like the learned philosopher and moralist Marcus Aurelius (161–180 C.E.), preserved Mediterranean civilization long enough for the Germanic tribes to become semicivilized before they finally succeeded in invading the Empire and rewriting all of Western history, a history that from the fifteenth century on increasingly has become the history of the world.

Let's not forget the tiny band of Spartans—the Greek warriors par excellence—who at Thermopylae in 480 B.C.E. defeated the Persian invasion of Europe, and saved the budding European democratic ideals.

In North America, Native American men lived and died with the Warrior energy informing even the smallest of their acts, living their lives nobly and with courage and with the capacity to endure great pain and hardship, defending their people against an overwhelming foe (the invading white people), and leaping into battle with the cry, "Today is a good day to die!"

Perhaps we need to look with an unbiased eye at the great twentieth-century warriors, among them, the generals Patton and MacArthur, great strategists, men of great courage, and men devoted to causes greater than their own personal survival. And then we may need to revalue the great Japanese samurai tradition and the ascetic, disciplined, utterly loyal men who built the nation of Japan, ensured the survival of its culture, and are today in business suits conquering the planet.

The Warrior energy, then, no matter what else it may be, is indeed universally present in us men and in the civilizations we create, defend, and extend. It is a vital ingredient in our world-building and plays an important role in extending the benefits of the highest human virtues and cultural achievements to all of humanity.

It is also true that this Warrior energy often goes awry. When this happens, the results are devastating. But we still have to ask ourselves why it is so present within us. What is the Warrior's function in the evolution of human life, and what is his purpose in the psyches of individual men? What are the Warrior's positive qualities? And how can they help us men in our personal lives and in our work?

The Warrior in His Fullness

The characteristics of the Warrior in his fullness amount to a total way of life, what the samurai called a *do* (pronounced "dough"). These characteristics constitute the Warrior's Dharma, Ma'at, or Tao, a spiritual or psychological path through life.

We have already mentioned aggressiveness as one of the Warrior's characteristics. Aggressiveness is a stance toward life that rouses, energizes, and motivates. It pushes us to take the offensive and to move out of a defensive or "holding" position about life's tasks and problems. The samurai advice was always to "leap" into battle with the full potential of *ki*, or "vital energy," at your disposal. The Japanese warrior tradition claimed that there is only one position in which to face the battle of life: frontally. And it also proclaimed that there was only one direction: forward.

In the famous opening scene of *Patton*, the general, in full battle gear, pearl-handled revolvers on his hips, is giving a motivational speech to his army. Patton warns his troops that he is not interested in their holding their position in battle. He says, "I don't want to get any messages saying that we are holding our position. . . . We are advancing constantly. . . . We are not interested in holding onto anything—except the enemy! We're going to hold onto him by the nose, and we're going to kick him in the ass! We're going to kick the hell out of him all the time, and we're going to go through him like crap through a goose!" Proper aggressiveness, in the right circumstances—circumstances strategically advantageous to the goal at hand—is already half the battle.

How does the Warrior know what aggressiveness is appropriate under the circumstances? He knows through clarity of thinking, through discernment. The Warrior is always alert. He is always awake. He is never sleeping through life. He knows how to focus his mind and his body. He is what the samurai called "mindful." He is a "hunter" in the Native American tradition. As Don Juan, the Yaqui Indian warrior-sorcerer in Carlos Castañeda's *Journey to Ixtlan,* says, a warrior knows what he wants, and he knows how to get it. As a function of his clarity of mind he is a strategist and a tactician. He can evaluate his circumstances accurately and then adapt himself to the "situation on the ground," as we say.

An example of this is the phenomenon of guerrilla warfare, an ancient tradition but one that has come into increasing use since the eighteenth century. The rebellious colonists adopted this technique in the American Revolutionary War. The Communists in China and later in Vietnam, under the guidance of the master strategist Ho Chi Minh, used it with stunning success to defeat the more cumbersome military operations of his enemies. Most recently, the Afghan resistance fighters used this strategy to drive the Soviet army out of their country. The Warrior knows when he has the force to defeat his opponent by conventional means and when he must adopt an unconventional strategy. He accurately assesses his own strength and skill. If he finds that a frontal assault will not work, he deflects his opponent's assault, spots the weakness in his flank, then "leaps" into battle. Here is a difference between the Warrior and the Hero. The Hero, as we've said, does not know his limitations; he is romantic about his invulnerability. The warrior, however, through his clarity of thinking realistically assesses his capacities and his limitations in any given situation.

In the Bible, King David, up against the superior force of the armies of Saul, at first avoided direct confrontation with Saul's troops, allowing

Achilles and Patroclus (Internal medallion of cup illustration by Greek Sosias Painter, ca. 500 B.C.E. Courtesy of Antikenmuseum Berlin, Staatliche Museen Preuffischer Kulturbesitz. Photo: Ute Jung.)

Saul to wear himself out pursuing him. David and his ragtag band were guerrillas, living off the land and moving fast. Then David, evaluating his situation clearly, fled Saul's kingdom and went over to the Philistine king. From this position, he had the force of thousands of Philistine soldiers behind him. He had put himself into position to checkmate Saul. Then, again through his accurate assessment of the situation at the time, David reentered Saul's kingdom, gathered his own troops, and waited for Saul's collapse. Sometimes, the maxim "Forward, always forward!" means shifting tactics. It means a flexibility of strategy that comes from razor-sharp evaluation.

Modern fencing uses this kind of flexibility. Not only does the fencer train his body, he trains his mind as well. He learns to think with lightning speed, to look for the unguarded points in his opponent's stances and lunges; then he parries, attacks, and scores his hits. A young college man reported that after he took up fencing his classroom performance improved. He was able to spot, with lightning-swift clarity, the major themes in a complex lecture, evaluate the weaknesses in the supporting arguments, challenge statements with a sharpness of vision and a self-confidence he'd never known before, and force his professors and fellow students to either talk sense or drop their arguments. He knew then what he wanted to learn. And he knew how to get it.

The Warrior traditions all affirm that, in addition to training, what enables a Warrior to reach clarity of thought is living with the awareness of his own imminent death. The Warrior knows the shortness of life and how fragile it is. A man under the guidance of the Warrior knows how few his days are. Rather than depressing him, this awareness leads him to an outpouring of life-force and to an intense experience of his life that is unknown to others. Every act counts. Each deed is done as if it were the last. The samurai swordsmen were taught to live their lives as if they were already dead. Castañeda's Don Juan taught that there is "no time" for anything but meaningful acts if we live with death as "our eternal companion."

There is no time for hesitation. This sense of the imminence of death energizes the man accessing the Warrior energy to take decisive action. This means that he engages life. He never withdraws from it. He doesn't "think too much," because thinking too much can lead to doubt, and doubt to hesitation, and hesitation to inaction. Inaction can lead to losing the battle. The man who is a Warrior avoids self-consciousness, as we usually define it. His actions become second nature. They become unconscious reflex actions. But they are actions he has trained for through the exercise of enormous self-discipline. This is how Marines are made. A good Marine is one who can make split-second decisions and then act decisively.

Part of what goes into acting decisively in any life situation, along with aggressiveness, clarity of thinking, the awareness of one's own death, is training. The Warrior energy is concerned with skill, power, and accuracy, and with control, both inner and outer, psychological and physical. The Warrior energy is concerned with training men to be "all that they can be"—in their thoughts, feelings, speech, and actions. Unlike the Hero's actions, the Warrior's actions are never overdone, never dramatic for the sake of drama; the Warrior never acts to reassure himself that he is as potent as he hopes he is. The Warrior never spends more energy than he absolutely has to. And he doesn't talk too much. Yul Brenner's character in the movie *The Magnificent Seven* is a study in trained self-control. He says little, moves with the physical control of a predator, attacks only the enemy, and has absolute mastery over the technology of his trade. That is another aspect of the Warrior's interest in skill, his mastery of the technology that enables him to reach his goal. He has developed skill with the "weapons" he uses to implement his decisions.

His control is, first of all, over his mind and his attitudes; if these are right, the body will follow. A man accessing the Warrior archetype has "a positive mental attitude," as they say in sales training. This means that he has an unconquerable spirit, that he has great courage, that he is fearless, that he takes responsibility for his actions, and that he has self-discipline. Discipline means that he has the rigor to develop control and mastery over his mind and over his body, and that he has the capacity to withstand pain, both psychological and physical. He is willing to suffer to achieve what he wants to achieve. "No pain, no gain," we say. Whether you are literally a hunter, crouched for hours in the same position in the chill early morning of the Kalahari waiting for your prey to come within range, or whether you're a triathlon trainee, a medical school student, an executive enduring the misguided attacks of your board members, or a husband trying to work out difficulties with your wife, you know that discipline of your mind and perhaps your body is essential.

The Warrior energy also shows what we can call a transpersonal commitment. His loyalty is to something—a cause, a god, a people, a task, a nation—larger than individuals, though that transpersonal loyalty may be focused through some important person, like a king. In the Arthurian stories, Lancelot, though fiercely devoted to Arthur and to Guinevere, is ultimately committed to the ideal of chivalry and to the God who lies behind such things as noble quests, "might for right," and the lifting up of the oppressed. Of course, because of his love for Guinevere, Lancelot unwittingly acts to destroy the object of his transpersonal commitment, Camelot. But he does so because he has encountered the paradoxically personal and transpersonal goal of romantic love. By then, he has already lost his access to the Warrior energies and has ceased being a knight.

This transpersonal commitment reveals a number of other characteristics of the Warrior energy. First, it makes all personal relationships relative, that is, it makes them less central than the transpersonal commitment. Thus the psyche of the man who is adequately accessing the Warrior is organized around his central commitment. This commitment eliminates a great deal of human pettiness. Living in the light of lofty ideals and spiritual realities such as God, democracy, communism, freedom, or any other worthy transpersonal commitment, so alters the focus of a man's life that petty squabbling and personal Ego concerns no longer matter much.

There is a story about a samurai attached to the household of a great lord. His lord had been murdered by a man from a rival house, and the samurai was sworn to avenge his lord's death. After tracking the assassin for some time, after great personal sacrifice and hardship, and after braving many dangers, the samurai found the murderer. He drew his sword to kill the man. But in that instant the assassin spit in his face. The samurai stepped back, sheathed his sword, and turned and walked away. Why?

He walked away because he was angry that he'd been spat on. He would have killed the assassin, in that moment, out of his own personal anger, not out of his commitment to the ideal his lord represented. His execution of the man would have been out of his Ego and his own feelings, not out of the Warrior within. So in order to be true to his warrior calling, he had to walk away and let the murderer live.

The Warrior's loyalty, then, and his sense of duty are to something beyond and other than himself and his own concerns. The Hero's loyalty, as we have seen, is really to himself—to impressing himself *with* himself and to impressing others. In this connection, too, the man accessing the Warrior is ascetic. He lives a life exactly the opposite of most human lives. He lives not to gratify his personal needs and wishes or his physical appetites but to hone himself into an efficient spiritual machine, trained to bear the unbearable in the service of the transpersonal goal. We know the legends of the founders of the great faiths Christianity and Buddhism. Jesus had to resist the temptations Satan pictured to him in the wilderness, and the Buddha had to endure his three temptations under the Bo Tree. These men were spiritual warriors.

Spiritual warriors abound in human history. The religion of Islam as a whole is built on Warrior energy. Mohammed was a warrior. His followers are, to this day, still drawing on Warrior energy as they wage *jihad* against the powers of evil as they define them. The God of Islam, even though he is addressed as "the Merciful" and "the Compassionate" is a Warrior God.

We see this same Warrior energy manifested in the Jesuit Order in Christianity, which for centuries taught self-negation for the sake of carrying God's message into the most hostile and dangerous areas of the world. The man who is a warrior is devoted to his cause, his God, his civilization, even unto death.

This devotion to the transpersonal ideal or goal even to the point of personal annihilation leads a man to another of the Warrior's characteristics. He is emotionally distant as long as he is in the Warrior. This does not mean that the man accessing the Warrior in his fullness is cruel, just that he does not make his decisions and implement them out of emotional relatedness to anyone or anything except his ideal. He is, as Don Juan says, "unavailable," or "inaccessible." As he says, "To be

inaccessible means that you touch the world around you sparingly,"
with emotional detachment. This attitude is part of the clarity of the
Warrior's thinking too. He looks at his tasks, his decisions, and his
actions dispassionately and unemotionally. Samurai training involved
the following kind of psychological exercise. Whenever, the teaching
went, you feel yourself frightened or despairing, don't say to yourself,
"I am afraid," or "I am despairing." Say, "There is someone who is
afraid," or "There is someone who is despairing. Now, what can he do
about this?" This detached way of experiencing a threatening situation
objectifies the situation and allows for a clearer and more strategically
advantageous view of it. The warrior is then able to act with less regard
for his personal feelings; he will act more forcefully, swiftly, and effi-
ciently with himself out of the way.

Often, in life, we need to "step back," we say, from a situation in
order to gain perspective, so that we can act. The Warrior needs room
to swing his sword. He needs separation from his opponents in the
outer world and from his own inner opponents in the form of negative
emotions. Boxers in the ring are separated by the referee when they get
too close to each other and engage each other in body-locks.

The Warrior is often a destroyer. But the positive Warrior energy
destroys only what needs to be destroyed in order for something new and
fresh, more alive and more virtuous to appear. Many things in our world
need destroying—corruption, tyranny, oppression, injustice, obsolete and
despotic systems of government, corporate hierarchies that get in the way
of the company's performance, unfulfilling life-styles and job situations,
bad marriages. And in the very act of destroying, often the Warrior energy
is building new civilizations, new commercial, artistic, and spiritual ven-
tures for humankind, new relationships.

When the Warrior energy is connected with the other mature masculine energies something truly splendid emerges. When the Warrior is
connected with the King, he is consciously stewarding the "realm,"
and his decisive actions, clarity of thinking, discipline, and courage are,
in fact, creative and generative. At this moment in history we need only
to think of Mikhail Gorbachev, warrior and king, struggling against the
inertia of the Soviet system, standing in the Center, making war on the
old and inefficient, generating the new and more vigorous, shepherd-

ing his people into a new era they themselves would not have the courage to face without his leadership, without his access to these two mature masculine energies.

The Warrior's interface with the Magician archetype is what enables him to achieve such mastery and control over himself and his "weapons." It is what allows him to channel and direct power to accomplish his goals.

His admixture with the Lover energy gives the Warrior compassion and a sense of connectedness with all things. The Lover is the masculine energy that brings him back into relatedness with human beings, in all their frailty and vulnerability. The Lover makes the man under the influence of the Warrior compassionate at the same time that he is doing his duty. Here we have the images, so dramatically captured for us on television, of the American GIs in Vietnam, after having bombed and strafed a Viet Cong village, carrying the children out on their hips and administering first aid to their wounded enemies. There's a powerful scene in the movie *Full-Metal Jacket*, in which several GIs have cornered and fatally wounded a Viet Cong sniper—a woman, as it turns out—who has killed several of their buddies. One of the characters feels compassion for his moments-ago enemy. She is writhing in agony, saying her prayers, preparing for death, and begging him to shoot her to put her out of her misery. The GI is torn between letting her die an agonizing death and helping her by finishing her off. In the end he shoots her, not out of anger but out of compassion.

Alliance with the Lover produces other humane influences in the Warrior energy. Marcus Aurelius was a philosopher. Winston Churchill was a painter. The Japanese artist-warrior Mishima was a poet. Even General Patton was a poet; he recited one of his eulogies to General Bradley at the site of the ancient North African battlefield upon which two thousand years earlier the Romans had defeated the Carthaginians. Patton claimed in his mystical poem that he had been there then, and had taken part in the battle.

When, however, the Warrior is operating on his own, unrelated to these other archetypes, the results for the mortal man accessing even the positive Warrior (the Warrior in his fullness) can be disastrous. As we have said, the Warrior in his pure form is emotionally detached; his transpersonal loyalty radically relativizes the importance of his human relationships. This is apparent in the Warrior's attitude toward sex. Women, for the Warrior, are not for relating to, for being intimate with. They are for fun. We've all heard the marching chant, "This is my rifle and this is my gun. This is for fighting, and this is for fun." This attitude explains the prevalence of prostitutes around military camps. It also explains the horrific tradition of the raping of conquered women.

Even if he has a family, the human warrior's devotion to other duties often leads to marital problems. The story of the lonely and rejected serviceman's wife is one we've seen time and time again in the movies. We need only recall Gordo Cooper's estrangement from his wife, Trudy, as portrayed in the movie *The Right Stuff.*

This same thing occurs outside the military as well, in the relationships and families of men whose professions call for a great deal of transpersonal devotion and long hours of disciplined work and self-sacrifice. Ministers, doctors, lawyers, politicians, dedicated salespeople, and many others often have emotionally devastating personal lives. Their wives and girlfriends often feel alienated and rejected, competing hopelessly with the man's "true love," his work. In addition, these men, true to the Warrior's sexual attitudes, often have affairs with their nurses, staffers, receptionists, secretaries, and other women who admire from a safe (sometimes not so safe) distance their masculine Warrior proficiency and dedication.

The Shadow Warrior: The Sadist and the Masochist

The Warrior energy's detachment from human relationships leads to real problems, as we're suggesting. These problems become enormously hurtful and destructive to a man when he is caught in the Warrior's bipolar Shadow. In the movie *The Great Santini*, Robert Duval plays a Marine fighter pilot who runs his family like a miniature Marine Corps. Most of his remarks and behavior toward his wife and children are depreciating, critical, commanding, and designed to put distance between him and the family members, who keep trying to relate to him lovingly. The destructiveness of this way of "relating" eventually becomes so obvious to everyone, especially to the older son, that there can no longer be any hiding from the fact that Santini's sometimes violent behavior results from his own inability to be tender and genuinely intimate. The "Great Santini," under the power of the Sadist, constantly has his emotional "sword" out, swinging at everyone—his daughters, who need to be treated like girls, not Marines; his oldest son, who needs his guidance and nurturing; and even his wife. There is a terrible scene in the kitchen when everything finally erupts; Santini physically attacks his wife, and then the kids attack him. Though detachment in itself is not necessarily bad, as we've said, it does leave the door open to the "demon" of cruelty. Because he is so vulnerable in this area of relatedness, the man under the influence of the Warrior needs urgently to have his mind and his feelings under control—not repressed, but under control. Otherwise, cruelty will sneak in the back door when he's not looking.

There are two kinds of cruelty, cruelty without passion and cruelty with passion. An example of the first kind is a practice the Nazis used in training the SS officer corps. The candidates for the corps would raise puppies, caring for them in every way, tending them when they were sick, feeding and grooming them, playing with them. Then, at an arbitrary moment decided upon by the trainer, these men were ordered to kill their puppies, and to do so with no sign of feeling. This training in unfeeling sadism evidently worked well, because these same men became the killing machines that manned the death camps—systematically, and without emotion, torturing and murdering millions of human beings while still thinking of themselves as "good fellows."

A contemporary image of the Warrior turned passionless killing machine is, of course, Darth Vader, from the *Star Wars* saga. It is alarming how many boys and adolescents identify with him. In this same connection, it is also alarming how many of these young men become members of survivalist and neo-Nazi groups.

Sometimes, though, the Sadist's cruelty is passionate. In mythology, we hear of avenging gods, and of the "wrath of God." In India, we see Shiva dancing the dance of universal destruction. In the Bible, Yahweh orders the fiery destruction of whole civilizations. Early in the Old Testament, we see this angry and vengeful God reducing the planet to mud through a great deluge, killing off nearly every living thing.

The Warrior as avenging spirit comes into us when we are very frightened and very angry. A kind of bloodlust, as it is called, comes over men in the stressful situation of actual combat, as well as in other stressful life situations. There is a scene in the movie *Apocalypse Now* in which the crew of the American gunboat, in a sampan boarding incident, panics and murders everyone on the sampan. Only after their fear has subsided do they realize that the people they have just murdered in their "battle frenzy" were innocent villagers going to market. A similar scene is presented in the movie *Platoon*, when the GIs open fire on a helpless Vietnamese village. This kind of savage outburst has haunted Americans ever since the incident at My Lai in which Lieutenant Calley, apparently terrified and angry, ordered the murder of every man, woman, and child in the village. That the sadistic Warrior actually loves such carnage and cruelty is made explicit again in *Patton*, when General Patton looks out over the smoking remains and the charred corpses of a great tank battle between the American and German forces and sighs, "God, I do love it so!"

Along with this passion for destruction and cruelty goes a hatred of the "weak," of the helpless and vulnerable (really the Sadist's own hidden Masochist). We've already mentioned the slapping incident in Patton's career. We see this same kind of sadism displayed in boot camp in the name of supposedly necessary "ritual humiliation" designed to deprive recruits of their individuality and put them under the power of a transpersonal devotion. Far too often, the drill sergeant's motives are the motives of the sadistic Warrior seeking to humiliate and violate the men put in his charge. And what can we make of the revolting practice of the Turkish army in World War I, when, after taking an Arab village, the soldiers delighted in cutting open pregnant women with their bayonets, ripping out their unborn babies, and hanging them around their necks?

It may seem at first unlikely, but the sadistic Warrior's cruelty is directly related to what is wrong with the Hero energy; there are similarities between the Shadow Warrior and the Hero. The Shadow Warrior carries into adulthood the adolescent insecurity, violent emotionalism, and the desperation of the Hero as he seeks to make a stand against the overwhelming power of the feminine, which always tends

Peter Paul Rubens: *Rape of Persephone*, 1636–1638. (©The Prado Museum, Madrid. Photo: ARXIU MAS.)

to evoke the masochistic, or cowardly, pole of the Hero's dysfunctional Shadow. The man under the influence of the Shadow Warrior's bipolarity, unsure of his legitimate phallic power, is still battling against what he experiences as the inordinately powerful feminine and against everything supposedly "soft" and relational. Even in adulthood, he still feels terrified that he will be swallowed up by it. His desperate fear of this leads him to wanton brutality.

We don't have far to look to see this destructive Warrior operating in our own lives. Sadly, we must acknowledge it in the workplace whenever a boss puts down, harasses, unjustly fires, or in many other ways mistreats his subordinates. We must also acknowledge the Sadist in our homes, in the appalling statistics of wife beating and child abuse.

Although we may all become vulnerable to the Sadistic Warrior at some time or another, there is a particular personality type that has this energy "in spades," as we say. This is the compulsive personality disorder. Compulsive personalities are workaholics, constantly with their noses to the grindstone. They have a tremendous capacity to endure pain, and they often manage to get an enormous amount of work done. But what is driving their nonstop engines is deep anxiety, the Hero's desperation. They have a very slim grasp on a sense of their own worthwhileness. They don't know what it is they really want, what they are missing and would like to have. They spend their lives "attacking" everything and everyone—their jobs, the life-tasks before them, themselves, and others. In the process, they are eaten alive by the Sadistic Warrior and soon reach "burnout."

We all know these people. They are the managers who stay at the office long after everyone else has gone home. And when they do finally go home, they seldom have a good night's sleep. These are the ministers, social workers, and therapists, the doctors and lawyers, who work literally day and night trying to plug the physical and psychological holes in other people, sacrificing their own lives for the sake of "saving" others. In the process, they really do a lot of harm—both to themselves and to those others who can't measure up to their impossible standards. They can't, of course, measure up to their own standards, so they mercilessly abuse themselves. If you have to admit to yourself that you really don't take care of yourself, that you don't care for your mental and physical well-being, then very probably the Shadow Warrior has got you.

As we've already suggested, men in some professions are especially endangered by dysfunctional Warrior energy. The military is an obvious example. What may not be so obvious is that revolutionaries and activists of all kinds may also fall into the sadistic pole of the Shadow Warrior. The old saying that we become what we hate applies here. It is a sad truth that leaders of revolutions—political, social, economic, the little revolutions within the corporation or the voluntary organization—once they have ousted the tyrants and oppressors (often by violence and terrorism) become themselves the new tyrants and the new oppressors. It was often said in the 1960s that the leaders of the peace movement were just as tyrannical and just as violent as those they fought against.

Salespeople and teachers, along with members of the many other professions already cited, can easily fall prey to compulsive, self-driven workaholic patterns. Eventually, they will snap. A car salesman entered analysis after years in the business as the top salesman, month after month, not only in his dealership but in the whole area. Every month, with enormous self-discipline and determination, he fought and scrapped to reach the top of the heap. Then one day something collapsed inside him. He had been sensing a gradual inner wearing down and a growing fatigue. And he had often talked about feeling "burned out." Then one morning he got up and realized that he was shaking all over and feeling terrified about going to work. Pretty soon he was not sleeping. He began having the overwhelming urge to cry at the most inappropriate times. He forced himself to go on for another several months. But finally the day arrived when everything at work—the showroom floor, the lot, his fellow workers, the customers—all seemed strangely unreal. He called his doctor and admitted himself to the hospital. The Sadistic Warrior had overpowered him. It had eaten him alive. Shortly after this, his wife left him, claiming with some apparent justification that he had been inattentive to her. He began therapy. In the course of his therapy he discovered the self-destructive power of his compulsiveness and how it worked to alienate him from others. And he resolved to turn over a new leaf.

Any profession that puts a great deal of pressure on a person to perform at his best all the time leaves us vulnerable to the shadow system of the Warrior. If we are not secure enough in our own inner structure, we will rely on our performance in the outer world to bolster our self-confidence. And because the need for this bolstering is so great, our behavior will gravitate toward the compulsive. The man who becomes obsessed with "succeeding" has already failed. He is desperately trying to repress the Masochist within him, yet he is already displaying masochistic and self-punishing behaviors.

The Masochist is the passive pole of the Warrior's Shadow, that "pushover" and "whipped puppy" that lies just beneath the Sadist's rageful displays. Men are right to fear the Coward within them, even if they don't have the sense to fear their macho exteriors. The Masochist projects Warrior energy onto others and causes a man to experience himself as powerless. The man possessed by the Masochist is unable to defend himself psychologically; he allows others (and himself) to push him around, to exceed the limits of what he can tolerate and still keep his self-respect, not to mention his psychological and physical health. All of us, no matter what our walk of life, can fall under the power of the Warrior's bipolar Shadow in any area of our lives. It may be that we don't know when to quit an impossible relationship, a circle of friends, or a frustrating job. We all know the saying "Quit while you're ahead," or "Learn to cut your losses." The compulsive personality, no matter what the danger signs, no matter how impossible the dream and unbeatable the foe, digs in and works harder, trying to get blood from a turnip and watching his gold turn to ashes in the end. If we are under the power of the Masochist, we will take far too much abuse for far too long and then explode in a sadistic outburst of verbal and even physical violence. This kind of oscillation between the active and passive poles of archetypal Shadows is characteristic of these dysfunctional systems.

Accessing the Warrior

If we are possessed by the active pole of the Warrior's Shadow, we will experience him in his sadistic form. We will abuse ourselves and others. If we feel that we are not in touch with the Warrior, however, we will be possessed by his passive pole. We will be cowardly masochists. We will dream but not be able to act decisively to make our dreams come true. We will lack vigor and be depressed. We will lack the capacity to endure the pain necessary for the accomplishment of any worthwhile goal. If we are in school, we won't get our assignments done; we won't get our papers written. If we are in sales and we are assigned a new territory, we'll sit and stare at the map and the list of all the contacts we need to make and not be able to pick up the phone and start calling. We will look at the task ahead and be defeated before we start. We won't be able to "leap into battle." If we are in politics, instead of being able to face the issues and the public concerns "frontally," we'll duck and dive, seeking a way out of direct confrontation. If we are underpaid on the job and figure there's money enough and we are good enough to rate a raise, we'll start down the hall to the boss's door, with fear and trembling, pause in indecision before it, and turn and walk away. As we do with all of the archetypes described in this book, we all need to ask ourselves not *if* we are possessed by one or both poles of their shadow systems, but *in what ways* we are failing to access properly the masculine energy potentials available to us.

If we are accessing the Warrior appropriately, we will be energetic, decisive, courageous, enduring, persevering, and loyal to some greater good beyond our own personal gain. At the same time, we need to be leavening the Warrior with the energies of the other mature masculine forms: the King, the Magician, and the Lover. If we are accessing the Warrior in the right way, we will, at the same time that we are "detached," be warm, compassionate, appreciative, and generative. We will care for ourselves and others. We will fight good fights in order to make the world a better and more fulfilling place for everyone and everything. Our war making will be for the creation of the new, the just, and the free.

7.   The MAGICIAN

There's a wonderful scene in the movie *The Right Stuff* in which "Gordo" Cooper reaches a tracking station in Australia's outback, from which he's going to monitor John Glenn's first orbital flight. As he pulls up to the station and steps out of his Land Rover, he meets a band of aborigines camping there. A young man steps forward. Gordo asks him, "Who are you guys?" The aborigine replies, "We're aborigines. Who are you?" Gordo says, "I'm an astronaut. I fly up there, among the moon and the stars." The young aborigine replies, "Oh, you too? See that bloke over there?" And he points to a wizened old man sitting under the shadow of an umbrella, his eyes squinting into the distance, as if he's staring into a reality others do not see. The young aborigine explains, "He knows too. He flies too. He knows."

Later that night, while Glenn is orbiting overhead, sparks flying from his deteriorating heat shield, the aborigines build a huge bonfire, swing their bullroarers, and waft the sparks from the fire skyward to join—so the movie editing shows it—the sparks from Glenn's capsule. By sympathetic magic, the channeling of hidden energies, the aborigine Magician helps give Glenn strength and aids him on his way.

We often mistakenly think that we are very different from our ancient ancestors, with our great knowledge and our amazing technology. But the origins of our knowledge and our technology lie in the minds of men like the old aborigine. He, and all those like him in tribal and ancient societies were accessing the Magician energy. And it is the Magician energy that drives our own modern civilization. Shamans, medicine men, wizards, witch doctors, brujos, inventors, scientists, doctors, lawyers, technicians—all these are accessing the same masculine energy pattern, no matter what age or culture they live in. Merlin, in the Arthurian stories, builds a Camelot of which our technology, psychology, and sociology still dream—regulated weather, an orderly and egalitarian society, the blessings of love and mutuality between people, and the recognized need to go questing for a supreme goal (in this case, the Holy Grail). Obe Wan Kanobe, in the *Star Wars* adventures, seeks to direct a renewal of his galaxy by a combination of his secret knowledge about "the Force" and the application of advanced technology.

The energies of the Magician archetype, wherever and whenever we encounter them, are twofold. The Magician is the knower and he is the master of technology. Furthermore, the man who is guided by the power of the Magician is able to fulfill these Magician functions in part by his use of ritual initiatory process. He is the "ritual elder" who guides the processes of transformation, both within and without.

The human magician is always an initiate himself, and one of his tasks is to initiate others. But of what is he an initiate? The Magician is an initiate of secret and hidden knowledge of all kinds. And this is the important point. All knowledge that takes special training to acquire is the province of the Magician energy. Whether you are an apprentice training to become a master electrician and unraveling the mysteries of high voltage; or a medical student, grinding away night and day, studying the secrets of the human body and using the available technologies to help your patients; or a would-be stockbroker or a student of high finance; or a trainee in one of the psychoanalytic schools, you are in exactly the same position as the apprentice shaman or witch doctor in tribal societies. You are spending large amounts of time, energy, and money in order to be initiated into rarefied realms of secret power. You are undergoing an ordeal testing your capacities to become a master of this power. And, as is true in all initiations, there is no guarantee of success.

The Magician is a universal archetype that has operated in the masculine psyche throughout history. It can be accessed today by modern men in their work and in their personal lives.

Historical Background

It is thought by some anthropologists that in the very ancient past the masculine energies of the King, the Warrior, the Magician, and the Lover were once inseparable and that one man—the "chief"—manifested all the functions of these archetypes in a holistic way. Since all four of these energies are in the masculine Self, and balanced there, it may be that the chief was the only one in the tribe who experienced himself as a whole man. Be that as it may, in the aboriginal societies that still exist today, these masculine energies are already somewhat distinct. There is the king, or chief. There are the chief's warriors. And there is the magician—the holy man, the witch doctor, the shaman. Whatever his title, his specialty is knowing something that others don't know. He knows, for instance, the secrets of the movements of the stars, the phases of the moon, the north-south swings of the sun. He knows when to plant and when to harvest, or when the herds will arrive next spring. He can predict the weather. He has knowledge of medicinal herbs and poisons. He understands the hidden dynamics of the human psyche and so can manipulate other human beings, for good or ill. He is the one who can effectively bless and curse. He understands the links between the unseen world of the spirits—the Divine World—and the world of human beings and nature. It is to him that people go with their questions, problems, pains, and diseases of the body and the mind. He is confessor and priest. He is the one who can think through the issues that are not obvious to other people. He is a seer and a prophet in the sense not only of predicting the future but also of seeing deeply.

This secret knowledge, of course, gives the magician an enormous amount of power. And because he has knowledge of the dynamics of energy flows and patterns in nature, in human individuals and societies, and among the gods—the deep unconscious forces—he is a master at containing and channeling power.

It was the magicians along the Tigris and Euphrates rivers, and along the Nile in Egypt, who created civilization as we know it. It was they who invented the secrets of written language, who discovered mathematics and engineering, astronomy, and law. The pharaohs had what the Bible calls wizards at their courts to advise them about all these things. The legendary Egyptian magician Imhotep (ca. 2800 B.C.E.) is credited with important discoveries in medicine, engineering, and other sciences. He designed and built the first great pyramid, the so-called Stepped Pyramid of Pharaoh Djoser. He was the Einstein and the Jonas Salk of his day.

One aspect of the magician's knowing, of his seeing into the depths not only of nature but of human beings was his capacity to deflate the arrogance, especially of kings, but also of any important public official. The Magician archetype in a man is his "bullshit detector"; it sees through denial and exercises discernment. He sees evil for what and where it is when it masquerades as goodness, as it so often does. In ancient times when a king became possessed by his angry feelings and wanted to punish a village that had refused to pay its taxes, the magician, with measured and reasoned thinking or with the stabbing blows of logic, would reawaken the king's conscience and good sense by releasing him from his tempestuous mood. The court magician, in effect, was the king's psychotherapist.

The prophet Nathan, King David's magician, performed this psychotherapeutic service for him on more than one occasion. But especially dramatic is the Bathsheba incident, which we've already referred to. After David had had his way with Bathsheba and had had her husband, Uriah, killed, Nathan came quietly into David's throne room and stood before him. Nathan then told David a story. He said that in a certain city there were two men, a rich man and a poor man. The poor man had only one little lamb. The rich man had many sheep. One day a traveler came to visit the rich man, and the rich man was obliged to give him a sumptuous feast. Instead of slaughtering one of his own sheep, he went to the poor man and took his one little lamb, killed it, and made the feast with it. King David, bursting with anger, proclaimed that whoever had done this thing deserved to die. Nathan answered, "You are the man." David repented. In the future, he was less inflated.

Merlin, King Arthur's magician, functioned much the same way for him. Merlin helped Arthur think things through and, in the process, sometimes deflated Arthur's arrogance. In the musical *Camelot*, and

T. H. White's magnificent *The Once and Future King*, upon which the play is based, Merlin frequently guides Arthur and, in effect, continually works to initiate him into appropriate ways of accessing the King energy. The result is that Arthur grows into fuller and fuller masculine maturity at the same time that he becomes a better king.

In late antiquity, coming out of the ancient Greek mystery religions and given new life by early Christianity, there was a movement called Gnosticism. *Gnosis* was the Greek word for "knowing" on a deep psychological or spiritual level. The Gnostics were knowers of the inner depths of the human psyche and the hidden dynamics of the universe. They were really proto–depth psychologists. They taught their initiates how to discover their own unconscious motives and drives, how to thread their way through the treacherous darkness of human delusions, and how, finally, to reach oneness with the Center that lies deep within. This Gnostic movement, concentrating as it did on insight and self-knowledge, was unpopular with the vast majority of early Christians, and it was persecuted out of existence by the Catholic church. Acquiring knowledge of whatever kind, but especially of the hidden workings of the psyche, is difficult and painful work that most of us have never wanted to do.

But in spite of the persecution of the magician class of early Christians, the Magician archetype could not, of course, be cast out; none of the instinctual energies of the psyche can be. This tradition of secret knowledge resurfaced in the Middle Ages in Europe as "alchemy." Most of us know that alchemy was on one level the attempt to make gold from common materials. On that level it was doomed to fail. But what most of us don't realize is that alchemy was also a spiritual technique for helping the alchemists themselves achieve insight, self-awareness, and personal transformation—that is, initiation into greater maturity.

In very large part, it was alchemy that gave birth to the modern sciences—certainly to the sciences of chemistry and physics. It is interesting to realize that our modern science, like the work of the ancient magicians, is also divided into two aspects. The first, "theoretical science," is the *knowing* aspect of the Magician energy. The second, "applied science," is the *technological* aspect of the Magician energy, the applied knowledge of how to contain and channel power.

Ours is, we believe, the age of the Magician, because it is a techno-logical age. It is an age of the Magician at least in his materialistic con-cern with understanding and having power over nature. But in terms of nonmaterialistic, psychological, or spiritual initiatory process, the Magician energy seems to be in short supply. We have already noted the absence of ritual elders who can initiate men into the deeper and more mature levels of masculine identity. Though technical schools and trade unions, professional associations, and many other institu-tions that express the Magician energy in the purely material world flourish and provide initiatory processes for those who seek to become "masters" in this sense, the Magician energy is not doing so well in the area of personal growth and transformation. Ours is an age, as we've said, of personal and gender identity chaos. And chaos is always the result of inadequate accessing of the Magician in some vital area of life.

Two sciences—subatomic physics and depth psychology—still do the work of the ancient magicians in a holistic way that brings together the material and the psychological sides of the Magician energy. Each seeks to know and then to at least partially control the very well-springs of the same hidden energies the ancients probed so profoundly.

Modern subatomic physics, it has been said, looks very much like Eastern mysticism as it approaches the intuited insights of Hinduism and Taoism. This new physics is discovering a microworld beneath our seemingly solid macroworld of sense perceptions. That unseen world of subatomic particles is very different from the macroworld we normally experience. In this hidden world beneath the surface of things, reality becomes very strange indeed. Particles and waves, so radically differ-ent in their properties in the macroworld, in the microworld are the same thing. A "particle" can appear to be in two separate places at the same time, without ever having divided. Matter loses its "solidity" and seems to be like gathered nodes of energy, concentrated in localized spots for more or less brief periods of time. Energy itself seems to arise out of an even more deeply concealed grid-like patterning of the void of space, which can no longer be viewed as "nothing." Particles arise from this underlying energy field like waves on the ocean, only to subside—or "decay"—again into the nothingness from which they came. Questions arise about time: what it is, what direction it's going.

Does it ever reverse? Do certain kinds of subatomic particles travel backward in time, and then reverse their direction to move in our time again? What is the origin of the universe, and its final fate? In the light of these new discoveries and questions, old questions resurface. What is the nature of being and of nonbeing? Are there, in fact, the other dimensions that mathematics predicts? In what ways might they be equivalent to what the ancient religions called other "planes" or "worlds"? Physicists have entered the realm of truly hidden and secret knowledge. And they are moving in a world of thought that looks very much like the world of the ancient magician.

The same is true of depth psychology. Jung, as he was making his first maps of the unconscious, was struck by the similarities between what he was discovering about the energy flows and the archetypal patterns in the human psyche and the quantum physics of, among others, Max Planck. Jung realized that he had stumbled onto a vast world that modern people had largely neglected, a world of living images and symbols that rose and fell like the waves of energy that seemed to account for our material universe. These archetypal realities, hidden in the deep void of the collective unconscious, seemed to be the building blocks of our thoughts and feelings and of our habitual patterns of behaviors and reactions, our macroworld of personality. For Jung, this collective unconscious looked very much like the unseen energy fields of the subatomic physicists, and to Jung both of these looked a lot like the mysterious underlying "pleroma" described by the Gnostics.

The conclusion of both modern physics and depth psychology is that things are not what they seem. What we experience as normal reality—about ourselves and nature—is only the tip of an iceberg that arises out of an unfathomable abyss. Knowledge of this hidden realm is the province of the Magician, and it is through the Magician energy that we will come to understand our lives with a degree of profundity not dreamed of for at least a thousand years of Western history.

There are indications that Jung thought of himself as a Magician. When asked once if he believed in God, he replied, in true Gnostic fashion, "I don't believe in God; I know." Some of his earliest followers have said that he imparted secrets to them that they could not reveal except to those initiated into the highest, or deepest, levels of psychic awareness.

This isn't mumbo jumbo. Every analyst knows that he or she must be careful how much to reveal to an analysand at any given time. The power of the unconscious energies is so great that if they are not controlled, contained, and channeled, if they are not accessed at just the right moment and in just the right dose, they may blow the Ego structure to bits. Too much power without the proper "transformers" and the right amount of "insulation" to contain it will overload the analysand's circuits and destroy him. The revelation of secret information must be measured out, because there are reasons for its having been hidden from the Ego in the first place.

There is another area in our modern world in which the psychological and spiritual knowledge and energy-channeling of the Magician archetype are being revived. This is the area of the so-called occult. There are many ritual magicians, from all walks of life—bankers, computer operators, housewives, chemical engineers, and many others—who do their "daylight" work like other people and then retire to their *real* work, mostly at night, in which they seek initiation into "higher planes." They contact what they call "entities" who teach them how to see more deeply and how to use the power that becomes available to them for good and for ill. These people—exactly like the ancient magicians—are concerned with knowledge of secret wisdom and powers and of the technological issues of containment (often through the insulating effects of "magic circles" and words of invocation and banishment) and of channeling (often through the use of the well-known "magic wand").

For all ritual process and for all deep knowing and controlling of energies of any kind, the issue of "sacred" space arises. Sacred space is the container of raw power—the "step-down transformer" that insulates and then channels the energies that are drawn into it. It is the reactor shield in the nuclear power plant. It is the sanctuary of the church. It is the hymns and the standard prayers, the invocations and blessings, used to invoke the Divine Power, and then to shield the believers from its raw intensity while at the same time providing them access to it.

There is a fascinating story in the Bible about this issue of containment and sacred space. King David and his army have recaptured the Ark of the Covenant—a sort of portable "generating station" for the power of Yahweh—from the Philistines. They are transporting it back to Jerusalem when the oxen pulling the cart with the Ark on it stumble. The Ark starts to go over. A soldier, walking beside the cart, instinctively reaches up and touches the Ark to steady it. He's immediately killed, because only the priests, the magicians, trained in the knowledge of how to handle the "reactor core" of the power of God, can touch it. They know the secret of insulation; they know how to contain and channel Yahweh's power on earth. The unfortunate soldier, for all his good intentions, did not.

In the movie *Raiders of the Lost Ark* we see a modern-day treatment of the generating power of the Ark theme. Here, Indiana Jones is racing the Nazis to find the Ark and then to use the enormous power of this ancient "technology." The Nazis get to it first. There is a wonderful scene in which the Nazi commander, robed in the appropriate ceremonial garb, is reciting the ritual invocations to activate the Ark's power. He's flipping the "on" switch. But he's evidently not a magician. Because once he's got the Ark going, he doesn't know how to contain the forces he has let loose. He can't find the "off" switch. The power of Yahweh gets loose, and, absent the magician as knower and technician, it atomizes the Nazi army.

A similar theme appears in a sequence in Walt Disney's *Fantasia*. Mickey Mouse, the sorcerer's apprentice, has been left with the job of mopping the workroom of his master—the sorcerer (magician). Rather than do the work in the conventional way, with elbow grease, he decides to use magic power. He activates the mop and bucket, and at first all goes well. But then the power he has released gets out of hand. He's only an apprentice, after all, and he doesn't know how to contain the energy he has set in motion. The mops and buckets begin to multiply. The scene becomes frantic, as unfortunate Mickey can't find the right words to stop this explosion of power. The mops and buckets keep dumping water into the room, until the apprentice is awash in a rising tide and threatened with drowning. Only the master's return saves the day.

With subatomic physics, all too often we have discovered belatedly that our knowledge and technology of containment have been inadequate. The Soviet disaster at Chernobyl is the most dramatic and the most unfortunate example.

The same thing has occurred in psychotherapy. Often, a therapist who has not been properly initiated and is not sufficiently adept himself—and is still an "apprentice" in some vital ways—sets off forces in the analysand that neither of them can contain. This issue of containment is one that has arisen time and time again in the context of group therapy, especially in the "encounter groups" of the sixties and seventies. Too often, neither the group participants nor the group leader had any real understanding of the forces that could be released. The leader had neither the knowledge nor the technological proficiency in psychological dynamics to control the process. The group would, as a result, turn negative, and "meltdown," first of individuals and then of the entire group, would occur.

The same thing happens at rock concerts, from time to time. The musicians invoke aggressive and volatile emotions in the audience, and then, if they are not accessing the Magician well enough, they are unable to contain and channel the energy. The audience becomes violent and may rampage through the concert hall and even out onto the streets in an orgy of destruction.

The Magician in His Fullness

What does all this mean for us men pursuing our own quests for personal happiness and for the life-enhancement of our loved ones, our companies, our causes, our peoples, our nations, and the world? What functions does the Magician energy of the mature masculine perform in our daily lives?

The Magician energy is the archetype of awareness and of insight, primarily, but also of knowledge of anything that is not immediately apparent or commonsensical. It is the archetype that governs what is called in psychology "the observing Ego."

While it is sometimes assumed in depth psychology that the Ego is secondary in importance to the unconscious, the Ego is in fact vital to our survival. It is only when it is possessed by, identified with, and inflated by another energy form—an archetype or a "complex" (an archetypal fragment, like the Tyrant)—that it malfunctions. Its proper role is to stand back and observe, to scan the horizon, to monitor the data coming in from both the outside and the inside and then, out of its wisdom—its knowledge of power, within and without, and its technical skill in channeling—make the necessary life decisions.

When the observing Ego is aligned with the masculine Self along an "Ego–Self axis," it is initiated into the secret wisdom of this Self. It is, in one sense, a servant of the masculine Self. But in another sense, it is the leader and the channeler of this Self's power. It is, then, a vital player in the personality as a whole.

The observing Ego is detached from the ordinary flow of daily events, feelings, and experiences. In a sense, it doesn't live life. It watches life, and it pushes the right buttons at the right times to access energy flows when they are needed. It is like the hydroelectric dam operator who watches his gauges and his computer screens for building pressures on the dam's surfaces and then decides whether or not to release water through the sluices.

The Magician archetype, in concert with the observing Ego, keeps us insulated from the overwhelming power of the other archetypes. It is the mathematician and the engineer in each of us that regulates the life functions of the psyche as a whole. It knows the enormous force of the psyche's inner dynamics and how to channel them for maximum benefit. It knows the unbelievable force of the "sun" within, and it knows how to channel that sun's energy for maximum benefit. The Magician pattern regulates the internal energy flows of the various archetypes for the benefit of our individual lives.

Many human magicians, in whatever profession or in whatever walk of life (occult practitioners as well), are consciously using their knowledge and technical proficiency for the benefit of others as well as themselves. Doctors, lawyers, priests, CEOs, plumbers and electricians, research scientists, psychologists, and many others are, when they are accessing the Magician energy appropriately, working to turn raw power to the advantage of others. This is true of the witch doctor and the shaman with their rattles, amulets, herbs, and incantations. And it is equally true of the medical research technicians who are looking for cures for our most deadly diseases.

The Magician energy is present in the Warrior archetype in the form of his clarity of thinking, which we've already discussed in some detail.

The Magician alone does not have the capacity to act. That is the Warrior's specialty. But he does have the capacity to think. Whenever we are faced with what seems like an impossible decision in our daily lives—who to promote in the company when there are difficult and complex political considerations to be taken into account, how to deal with our son's lack of motivation in school, how to design a particular home so as to meet both the clients' specifications and the city codes, how much to reveal to an analysand about the meaning of his dreams when we see him headed for a crisis, even how to budget in tight financial circumstances—whenever we do these things, make these decisions, with careful and insightful deliberation, we are accessing the Magician.

The Magician, then, is the archetype of thoughtfulness and reflection. And, because of that, it is also the energy of introversion. What we mean by introversion is not shyness or timidity but rather the capacity to detach from the inner and outer storms and to connect with deep inner truths and resources. Introverts, in this sense, live much more out of their centers than other people do. The Magician energy, in aiding the formation of the Ego–Self axis, is immovable in its stability, centeredness, and emotional detachment. It is not easily pushed and pulled around.

The Magician often comes on line in a crisis. A middle-aged man reported to us what happened to him in a recent car accident. It was winter, and he was coming down a hill. There was a car ahead of him stopped at a stop sign at the bottom of the hill. Suddenly, in the middle of his normal braking procedures, he hit a patch of ice. His brakes locked and his car took off down the hill like a rocket. He felt panic as he slid straight for the rear bumper of the other car. Then something remarkable happened: a shift of consciousness. All of a sudden, everything seemed to move in slow motion. The man felt calm and steady. He now had the "time" to sort through what few options he had. It was as if a computer took over, some other kind of intelligence within him. And a "voice" from within told him to release the brake pedal, pump it a few times, and steer as best he could to the right. That way, he would hit the car below him at an angle, minimizing the impact, and more or less harmlessly come to a stop in the soft, snowy embankment at the side of the road. The man executed these maneuvers successfully.

Hermes Trismegistus, Sophic Sulphur and Mercury (Engraving from *Symbola Aureae Mensae*, 1617, courtesy of the British Library, London.)

What we think he was reporting was sudden access to the Magician energy, an energy whose detached "knowledge" of various possible outcomes and understanding of lines of force (of containment and channeling) could help him, through technical proficiency, make the best of a bad situation.

If we think for a moment about all the areas of our lives in which clear, careful thinking based on inner wisdom and technical proficiency would help, then we realize our need to properly access the Magician.

Often, in difficult situations like this one people are drawn into some kind of space and time frame that can be called "sacred," because it is so different from the space and time we normally experience. The driver in our example suddenly found himself in an inner space and time (the slow-motion effect he described) far different from his panic and fear. This "sacred" space is something men who are guided by the Magician know well. These men may actually put themselves into that "space" deliberately, much like ritual magicians who draw their magic circles and recite their incantations. They enter this space by listening to certain musical pieces, by tending to a hobby, by taking long walks in the woods, by meditating on certain themes and mental pictures, and by many other methods. When they enter this sacred space within they can be in touch with the Magician; they can emerge from the inner space seeing what they need to do about a problem and knowing how to do it.

We believe that the many ways in which the Magician has appeared in history and in which he appears among men today are mere fragments of a once-whole image. That primordial Magician in men has manifested itself most fully in what anthropologists refer to as the shaman. The shaman in traditional societies was the healer, the one who restored life, who found lost souls, and who discovered the hidden causes of misfortune. He was the one who restored wholeness and fullness of being to both individuals and communities. Indeed, the Magician energy today still has the same ultimate aim. The Magician, and the shaman as his fullest human vessel, aims at fullness of being for all things, through the compassionate application of knowledge and technology.

The Shadow Magician:
The Manipulator and the Denying "Innocent" One

As positive as the Magician archetype is, like all the other forms of the mature masculine energy potentials, it too has a shadow side. If ours is an age of the Magician, then it is also an age of the bipolar Shadow Magician. We need only to think about the mushrooming problem of toxic wastes poisoning and blighting our planet's environment. The "mops and buckets" of the sorcerer's apprentice are proliferating as the ozone layer yawns open, as the oceans throw back our trash, as wildlife perishes (many species to complete extinction), as the Brazilian rain forests come down, not only destroying the ecology of Brazil but threatening the globe's capacity to produce enough oxygen to sustain most life forms. It was the Shadow Magician that handed us in the darkest days of World War II, not only the technology of the death camps, but also the doomsday weapon that still hangs over all our heads. Mastery over nature, a proper function of the Magician, is running amuck, and with incalculable results that we are already beginning to feel. Behind the propaganda ministries, the controlled press briefings, the censored news, and the artificially orchestrated political rallies lies the face of the Magician as Manipulator.

The active pole of the Shadow Magician is, in a special sense, a "power Shadow." A man under this Shadow doesn't guide others, as a Magician does; he directs them in ways they cannot see. His interest is not in initiating others by graduated degrees—degrees that they can integrate and handle—into better, happier, and more fulfilled lives. Rather, the Manipulator maneuvers people by withholding from them information they may need for their own well-being. He charges heavily for the little information he does give, which is usually just enough to demonstrate his superiority and his great learning. The Shadow Magician is not only detached, he is also cruel.

Regrettably, a good example of this can be found in our graduate schools. A number of graduate students—bright, gifted, and hardworking—have told us of Shadow Magician experiences with their professors. Rather than accessing the Magician appropriately and thus serving as guides for these young people's initiation into the eseoteric realm of advanced studies, these men habitually attacked their students, seeking to crush their enthusiasm. Unfortunately, this scenario is repeated all too frequently in educational institutions on all levels—from kindergarten to medical school, from high school to trade school.

Many men involved in modern medicine demonstrate this power Shadow too. It is well known that the best money in medicine is made by the specialist, who is an initiate into rarefied fields of knowledge. There are, no doubt, many medical specialists who are genuinely interested in their patients' well-being. But many of these men will not tell their patients important details about what is wrong with them. Especially in the field of oncology, doctors routinely withhold vital information that would allow their patients to prepare themselves and their families for the treatment ordeal to come as well as for the possibility of death. Furthermore, the soaring costs of medicine—especially of exotic equipment and procedures—testify to the greed not only for power (the power that secret knowledge brings its possessor) but also for material wealth that men possessed by the Manipulator fall victim to. These men are using their secret knowledge for their own purposes first and only secondarily, if at all, for the benefit of others.

The growing complexity of law and the coded language of legal proceedings and documents—whatever else they may be intended for—clearly proclaim to the general public, "We in the legal profession have access to hidden knowledge that can make or break you. And after we've charged you an outrageous fee for our services, you may, or may not, benefit from our magic."

Too often, as well, in the consulting room, the therapist will withhold information that the client needs in order to get better and will subtly, or not so subtly, communicate to the client, "I am the keeper of great wisdom and secret knowledge, a wisdom and a knowledge you need in order to become well. I have it. Try to get it from me. And by the way, leave your check with my secretary on the way out."

This withholding and secretiveness for the purpose of self-aggrandizement are also to be seen on "Madison Avenue." The wholesale manipulation of the public psyche by the advertisers to feed the greed and status-seeking of the companies they work for, even to the point of outright lying, displays a cynical detachment from the realm of

The mad scientist (From *Werewolf of London*. Photo courtesy of Culver Pictures, Inc.)

genuine relatedness that is every bit as destructive and self-serving as anything done by the propaganda ministries of totalitarian governments. Through their skillful use of images and symbols that appeal to the wounds of their fellow human beings, these charlatans rattle the beads and shake the feathers of the black magic practitioner, the evil sorcerer, the voodoo witch doctor.

The man under the power of the Manipulator not only hurts others with his cynical detachment from the world of human values and his subliminal technologies of manipulation, he also hurts himself. This is the man who thinks too much, who stands back from his life and never lives it. He is caught in a web of pros and cons about his decisions and lost in a labyrinth of reflective meanderings from which he cannot extricate himself. He is afraid to live, to "leap into battle." He can only sit on his rock and think. The years pass. He wonders where the time has gone. And he ends by regretting a life of sterility. He is a voyeur, an armchair adventurer. In the world of academia, he is a hairsplitter. In his fear of making the wrong decision, he makes none. In his fear of living, he also cannot participate in the joy and pleasure that other people experience in their *lived* lives. If he is withholding from others, and not sharing what he knows, he eventually feels isolated and lonely. To the extent that he has hurt others with his knowledge and his technology— in whatever field and in whatever way—by cutting himself off from living relatedness with other human beings, he has cut off his own soul.

A number of years ago there was a *Twilight Zone* story about a man possessed by the Shadow Magician in this way. This man loved to read, and believed himself to be superior to his fellow human beings. He rebuffed others' attempts to get to know him and to get him to share his rather considerable knowledge. Then one day there was a nuclear war, and this man was the last human being left alive on the earth. Rather than being devastated about this development, he was elated, and he hurried to the nearest library. There he found the building in ruins and thousands of books scattered on the ground. In great joy, he bent over to look at the first heap of them, and dropped his glasses in the rubble. The lenses shattered.

Whenever we are detached, unrelated, and withholding when what we know could help others, whenever we use our knowledge as a weapon to belittle and control others or to bolster our status or wealth at others' expense, we are identified with the Shadow Magician as Manipulator. We are doing black magic, damaging ourselves as well as those who could benefit from our wisdom.

The passive pole of the Magician's Shadow is what we are calling the Naive, or "Innocent" One. The "Innocent" One is a carryover from childhood into adulthood of the passive pole of the Precocious Child's Shadow—the Dummy. The "Innocent" One as well. He wants the power and status that traditionally come to the man who is a magician, at least in the societally sanctioned fields. But he doesn't want to take the responsibilities that belong to a true magician. He does not want to share and to teach. He does not want the task of helping others in the careful, step-by-step way that is a necessary part of every initiation. He does not want to be a steward of sacred space. He doesn't want to know himself, and he certainly doesn't want to make the great effort necessary to become skilled at containing and channeling power in constructive ways. He wants to learn just enough to derail those who *are* making worthwhile efforts. While he is protesting the innocence of his hidden power motives, the man possessed by the "Innocent" One, "too good" to make any real efforts himself, blocks others and seeks their downfall. Whereas the Trickster plays his tricks in part for the sake of revealing the truth, the "Innocent" One *hides* truth for the sake of achieving and maintaining his own precarious status. While the Trickster aims at the necessary deflation of our grandiosity, the Shadow Magician, as both Manipulator and "Innocent" One, works at deflating us when such deflation is not only unnecessary but harmful as well.

The "Innocent" One's underlying motivations come from envy of those who act, who live, who want to share. Because he is envious of life, he is also afraid that people will discover his lack of life energy and throw him off his very wobbly pedestal. His detachment and his "impressive behavior," his deflating remarks, his hostility toward questions, even his accumulated expertise, are all designed to cover his real inner desolation and hide his actual lifelessness and irresponsibility from the world.

The man possessed by the "Innocent" One commits both sins of commission and sins of omission but hides his hostile motives behind an impenetrable wall of feigned naïveté. Such men are slippery and illusive. They do not allow us to engage them frontally with our Warrior energy. They parry our attempts to confront them, thus keeping us off balance by seducing us into an endless process of questioning our own intuitions about their behavior. If we challenge their "innocence," they will often react with a show of tear-jerking bewilderment and leave us to stew in our own juices. We may even feel ashamed of ourselves for having attributed base motives to them and conclude that we must be paranoid. But we will not be able to escape the uneasy feeling that we have been manipulated. And, in that feeling, we will have detected the *active* pole of the Magician's Shadow behind the smoke-screen of "innocence."

Accessing the Magician

If we are possessed by the Manipulator, we will be in the grip of the Magician's power Shadow. If we feel that we are out of touch with the Magician in his fullness, we will be caught in the dishonest and denying passive pole of his Shadow. In this case, we will not have much sense of our own inner structure, of our own calmness and clearheadedness. We won't have a sense of inner security, and we won't feel that we can trust our thinking processes. We won't be able to detach from our emotions and our problems. We're likely to experience inner chaos and to be vulnerable to outside pressures that will push and pull us in many different directions. We will act in a passive-aggressive way toward others, but claim to be innocent of any ill intentions.

One of the hardest things to do as a counselor or therapist is to get clients to separate their Egos from their emotions without at the same time repressing the emotions. There is a really good psychological exercise for doing this that can help; it's called *focusing*, originated by Eugene Gendlin. We ask our clients, when they sense the onset of strong emotions—strong fear, envy, anger, despair—to sit down in an "observation" chair and as the feelings come up imagine placing them in a stack in the middle of the room. Each one should be placed on the stack carefully, and we can sit back and watch the feeling—its color, its shape, and the nuances of its emotional tones. We ask our clients to watch their feelings—not judging them or putting them down but, rather, observing them. "Oh, there you are again! That's what you look like!" If the feelings are in the middle of the room, where the Ego can see them, they are not being repressed. Then, when the force of the feelings has passed, we ask our clients to banish them.

What this exercise does is help the client strengthen his connection with the Magician energy. It is the Magician that watches and thinks. It is the Magician that enables the Ego to place the feelings in an orderly stack. The emotional energies, thus contained, eventually lose their power. Finally, the strengthened Ego may be able to take this raw emotive energy and transform it into useful and life-enhancing forms of Self-expression.

Another exercise helped a young man access his Magician energy. This young man was terrorized almost nightly by dreams about tornadoes coming at him. The huge, black funnel clouds would come right up to him as he cringed under a tree in the backyard of his childhood home. He had no idea what this meant. During the course of his therapy he came to realize that his unconscious, through these tornado dreams, was picturing his childhood rage to him. His parents had been alcoholics, and he had been made responsible for running the household and taking care of them. Not only that, but he had been sexually abused repeatedly by one of his uncles. His childhood rage was enormous, and it was now showing itself in all its ferocity in his dreams. These uncontainable storms rampaging through this young man's inner countryside were tearing up his professional and personal life. He was deeply depressed.

Because the young man was something of an artist, his therapist suggested to him that he draw a picture of the tornadoes. He then was to draw a picture of the tornadoes in a lead-shielded container, so that his rage would just whirl around and around like the magnetic coil in an electric generator. Next, he was to draw power lines and transformers coming out of the container and going to the streetlights, the houses, and the factories—whatever needed this energy.

As soon as he did this, the young man's life began to change. He found the strength to quit his job. He had always wanted to work in children's theater. Suddenly, almost out of the blue, job offers for this kind of work started coming in. The tremendous energy of his raw childhood rage, now contained and channeled into the "lights" and "factories" of his present life, was acting as a power station for his new way of living. The "black magic" of his wild and chaotic anger was now the "white magic" of "electricity," "illuminating" his life.

What the therapist had done by suggesting the drawing was to enable his client to draw upon the Magician in his fullness in order to contain and to channel primal emotions. If we are accessing the Magician appropriately we will be adding to our professional and personal lives a dimension of clearsightedness, of deep understanding and reflection about ourselves and others, and technical skill in our outer work and in our inner handling of psychological forces. As we access the Magician, we need to regulate this energy with the other three archetypes of mature masculinity patterns. None of them, as we've suggested, works well alone; we need to mix with the Magician the King's concern for generativity and generosity, the Warrior's ability to act decisively and with courage, and the Lover's deep and convinced connectedness to all things. We will then be using our knowledge, our containment, and our channeling of energy flows for human benefit and, perhaps, for the enhancement of the whole planet.

8.   *The LOVER*

The Elephanta Caves, on an island in the Arabian Sea just off the coast of Bombay, India, are a spectacular sight even from a distance. These are the original "Temples of Doom" of *Indiana Jones* fame. They are set in a steep, heavily forested mountainside, the trees coming down to the water's edge. Monkeys scamper through the underbrush and swing, howling and screeching, through the tree tops.

Once you are inside, these temple-complex caverns open up into dusky, mysterious splendor. And there, by the light of hundreds of glimmering candles, towering in the gloom, carved out of the living rock, is a huge representation of the great phallus of the Indian god Shiva, the Creator and Destroyer of the world. This image is so power-ful, so charged with life-force for the faithful, that day and night the cave-temple hums with the comings and goings of thousands of pil-grims and echoes with their songs and chants. The worshiper is caught in a mood of utter fascination by this graphic portrayal of the divine masculine and responds with a hushed "yes" of recognition.

The ancient Greeks had a god, Priapus, whose phallus was so large he had to carry it ahead of him in a wheelbarrow. The Egyptians hon-ored the god Osiris in the form of the *djed* pillar. In their traditional fer-tility festivals, the Japanese still dance with huge artificial phalluses that are intended to evoke the procreative powers of nature.

The erect penis is, of course, a sexual symbol. But it is also a symbol of the life-force itself. For ancient peoples, blood was the carrier of spirit, energy, the soul. And when the blood stood the penis erect, it was incarnating spirit into flesh. The life-force—always divine—was entering the profane world of matter and of human life. The result of this union of the human and the divine, of the world and God, was always creative and energizing. From this union new life and new forms, new combinations of opportunities and possibilities, were born.

There are many forms of love. The ancient Greeks spoke of *agape*, nonerotic love, what the Bible calls "brotherly love." They spoke of *eros* both in the narrow sense of phallic or sexual love and in the wider sense of love as the bonding and uniting urge of all things. The Romans spoke of *amor*, the complete union of one body and soul with another body and soul. These forms, and all other forms of love (for the most part varieties of these), are the living expression of the Lover energy in human life.

Jungians often use the name of the Greek god Eros to talk about the Lover energy. They also use the Latin term *libido*. By these terms they mean not just sexual appetites but a general appetite for life.

We believe that the Lover, by whatever name, is the primal energy pattern of what we could call vividness, aliveness, and passion. It lives through the great primal hungers of our species for sex, food, well-being, reproduction, creative adaptation to life's hardships, and ultimately a sense of meaning, without which human beings cannot go on with their lives. The Lover's drive is to satisfy those hungers.

The Lover archetype is primary to the psyche also because it is the energy of sensitivity to the outer environment. It expresses what Jungians call the "sensation function," the function of the psyche that is trained in on all the details of sensory experience, the function that notices colors and forms, sounds, tactile sensations, and smells. The Lover also monitors the changing textures of the inner psychological world as it responds to incoming sensory impressions. We can easily see the survival value of this energy potential for our distant, rodentlike ancestors, who struggled for survival in a dangerous world.

Whatever the primeval background, how does the Lover show up in men today? How does he help us to survive and even to flourish? What are the Lover's characteristics?

The Lover in His Fullness

The Lover is the archetype of play and of "display," of healthy embodiment, of being in the world of sensuous pleasure and in one's own body *without shame*. Thus, the Lover is *deeply sensual*—sensually aware and sensitive to the physical world in all its splendor. The Lover is related and connected to them all, drawn into them through his sensitivity. His sensitivity leads him to feel compassionately and empathetically united with them. For the man accessing the Lover, all things are bound to each other in mysterious ways. He sees, as we say, "the world in a grain of sand." This is the consciousness that knew long before the invention of holography that we live, in fact, in a "holographic" universe—one in which every part reflects every other in immediate and sympathetic union. It isn't just that the Lover energy *sees* the world in a grain of sand. He *feels* that this is so.

A young boy entered psychotherapy at the insistence of his parents, because, as they said, he was very "strange." He was, they said, spending too much time alone. What this boy reported, when asked about his supposed "strangeness," was that he would go on long walks in the forest until he found a secluded spot. He would sit down on the ground and watch the ants and other insects making their tortuous ways through the blades of grass, the fallen leaves, and the other tiny plants of the forest floor. Then, he said, he would begin to feel what the world is like for the ants. He would imagine himself as an ant. He could *feel* the sensations of the ant as it climbed over the pebbles (to him, huge rocks) and swayed precariously on the ends of leaves.

Perhaps even more remarkable, the boy reported that he could feel what it was like to be the lichen on the trees and the cool, damp moss on the fallen logs. He experienced the hunger, and the joy, the suffering and the satisfaction, of the whole animal and plant world.

This boy was, in our view, accessing the Lover in a powerful way. He was instinctively *empathizing* with the world of things around him. Perhaps he *was* really feeling, as he believed he was, the actual experiences of those things.

We believe that the man accessing the Lover is open to a "collective unconscious," perhaps even vaster than that which Jung proposed. Jung's collective unconscious is the "unconscious" of human beings as an entire species and contains, as Jung said, the unconscious memories of all that has ever happened in the lives of all the people that have ever lived. But if, as Jung suggested, the collective unconscious appears to be limitless, why stop here? What if the collective unconscious is vast enough to include the impressions and sensations of all living things? Perhaps, indeed, it includes what some scientists are now calling "primary awareness" even in plants.

This idea that there is a universal consciousness is reflected in Obe Wan Kanobe of the *Star Wars* series, who is deeply sensitive to and empathic toward the whole of his galaxy and feels any subtle changes in "the Force." Eastern philosophers have said that we are like waves on the surface of this vast sea. The Lover energy has immediate and intimate contact with this underlying "oceanic" connectedness.

Along with sensitivity to all inner and outer things comes passion. The Lover's connectedness is not primarily intellectual. It is through feeling. The primal hungers are felt passionately in all of us, at least beneath the surface. But the Lover knows this with a deep knowing. Being close to the unconscious means being close to the "fire"—to the fires of life and, on the biological level, to the fires of the life-engendering metabolic processes. Love, as we all know, is "hot," often "too hot to handle."

The man under the influence of the Lover wants to touch and be touched. He wants to touch everything physically and emotionally, and he wants to be touched by everything. He recognizes no boundaries. He wants to live out the connectedness he feels with the world inside, in the context of his powerful feelings, and outside, in the context of his relationships with other people. Ultimately, he wants to experience the world of sensual experience in its totality.

He has what is known as an aesthetic consciousness. He experiences everything, no matter what it is, aesthetically. All of life is art to him and evokes subtly nuanced feelings. The nomads of the Kalahari are Lovers. They are aesthetically attuned to everything in their environment. They see hundreds of colors in their desert world, subtle nuances of light and shadow and shades of what to us are simply browns or tans.

Lovers (Mithuna) (India: Madhya Pradesh, Khajuraho style, eleventh century C.E., courtesy of Cleveland Museum of Art, Leonard C. Hanna, Jr. Fund, CMA 82.64.)

The Lover energy, arising as it does out of the Oedipal Child, is also the source of spirituality—especially of what we call mysticism. In the mystical tradition, which underlies and is present in all the world's religions, the Lover energy, through the mystics, intuits the ultimate Oneness of all that is and actively seeks to experience that Oneness in daily life, while it still dwells in a mortal, finite man.

The same boy who could imagine himself as an ant also reported what we could see as the beginnings of mystical experience in his account of a peculiar feeling he had on certain occasions at a YMCA camp one summer. Once a week, the campers would be roused from their beds late at night and trekked along obscure forest paths in the pitch blackness to a central clearing, there to watch a reenactment of ancient Native American songs and dances. This boy said that often, as he was snaking his way along behind the other boys from his cabin, he would have the almost uncontrollable urge to open his arms wide to the darkness and to fly into it, feeling the trees tear through his "spiritual body" with no pain, just a feeling of ecstasy. He said he felt like he wanted to be "one" with the mystery of the dark unknown and with the threatening yet strangely reassuring night forest. These kinds of sensations are exactly what the mystics of the world's religions describe when they talk about their urge to become One with the Mystery.

For the man accessing the Lover, ultimately everything in life is experienced this way. While feeling the pain and the poignancy of the world, he feels great joy as well. He feels joy and delight in all the sensory experiences of life. He may know, for example, the joy of opening a cigar humidor and smelling the exotic aromas of the tobaccos. He may also be sensitive to music. He may feel exquisitely the eerie thrumming of the Indian sitar, the swelling of a great symphony, or the ascetic thunk of an Arab clay drum.

Writing may be a sensuous experience for him. When we have asked writers why so many of them feel that they have to smoke when they sit down to their typewriters, they have told us that smoking relaxes them by opening up their senses to impressions, feelings, the nuances of words. They feel deeply connected by doing this with what they call "the earth," or "the world." Inside and outside come together in one continuous whole, and they are able to create.

Languages—the different sounds and the subtle meanings of words—will be approached through the Lover's emotional appreciation. Other people may learn languages in a mechanical way, but men accessing the Lover learn them by feeling them.

Even highly abstract thoughts, like those of philosophy, theology, or the sciences, are felt through the senses. Alfred North Whitehead, the great twentieth-century philosopher and mathematician, makes this clear in his writings, at once technical and deeply feeling-toned, even sensual. And a professor in higher mathematics reported being able to *feel*, as he put it, what the "fourth dimension" is like.

The man profoundly in touch with the Lover energy experiences his work, and the people on the job with him, through this aesthetic consciousness. He can "read" people like a book. He is often excruciatingly sensitive to their shifts in mood and can feel their hidden motives. This can be a very painful experience indeed.

The Lover is not, then, only the archetype of the joy of life. In his capacity to feel at one with others and with the world, he must also feel their pain. Other people may be able to avoid pain, but the man in touch with the Lover must endure it. He feels the painfulness of being alive—both for himself and for others. Here, we have the image of Jesus weeping—for his city, Jerusalem, for his disciples, for all of humanity—and taking the sorrows of the world upon himself as the "man of sorrows, one acquainted with grief," as the Bible says.

We *all* know that love brings both pain and joy. Our realization that this is profoundly and unalterably true is archetypally based. Paul, in his famous "Hymn to Love," which proclaims the characteristics of authentic love, says that "love bears all things" and "endures all things." And so it does. The troubadours of the late Middle Ages in Europe sang of the exquisite "pain of love" that simply is an inescapable part of its power.

The man under the influence of the Lover does not want to stop at socially created boundaries. He stands against the artificiality of such things. His life is often unconventional and "messy"—the artist's studio, the creative scholar's study, the "go for it" boss's desk. Consequently, because he is opposed to "law," in this broad sense, we see enacted in his life of confrontation with the conventional the old tension between sensuality and morality, between love and duty, between, as Joseph Campbell poetically describes it, "amor and Roma"—"amor" standing for passionate experience and "Roma" standing for duty and responsibility to law and order.

The Lover energy is thus utterly opposed—at least at first glance—to the other energies of the mature masculine. His interests are the opposite of the Warrior's, the Magician's, and the King's concerns for boundaries, containment, order, and discipline. What is true within each man's psyche is true in the panorama of history and cultures as well.

Cultural Background

In the history of our religions and the cultures that flow from them, we can see this pattern of tension between the Lover and the other archetypes of the mature masculine. Christianity, Judaism, and Islam—what are called moral, or ethical, religions—have all persecuted the Lover. Christianity has taught more or less consistently that the world—the very object of the Lover's devotion—is evil, that the Lord of this world is Satan, and that it is he who is the source of the sensuous pleasures (the foremost of which is sex) that Christians must avoid. The Church has often stood opposed to artists, innovators, and creators. In the late Roman period, when the Church first gained power, one of the first things it did was close the theaters. Soon after, it closed the brothels and forbade the displaying of pornographic art. There was no room for the Lover, not, at least, in his erotic expression.

Following the ancient Hebrew practice, the Church also persecuted psychics and mediums, people who along with artists and others live very close to the image-making unconscious, and, hence, to the Lover. Here is a source of the witch burnings of the Middle Ages. Some of the witches, as far as the Church was concerned, were not only psychic— that is, deeply intuitive and sensitive to impressions from the inner world of nuanced feelings—but they were also nature worshipers. Because the Church labeled the world of nature evil, the witches were believed to be worshipers of Satan, the Lover.

To this day, many Christians are still scandalized by the one truly erotic book in the Bible: the Song of Solomon. It is a series of love poems (based on ancient Canaanite fertility rituals) and it is pornographic in the best sense of the word. It describes the amor—the physical and spiritual bonding—between a man and a woman. The only way that these moralistic Christians can accept the Song of Solomon is by interpreting it as an allegory of "Christ's love for the Church."

Archetypes cannot be banished or wished away. The Lover crept back into Christianity in the form of Christian mysticism, through romantic and sentimental pictures of a "sweet Jesus, meek and mild," and through the hymnal. If we think for a moment about the erotic undertones in hymns such as "In the Garden," "Love Lifted Me," and "Jesus, Lover of My Soul," to mention just a few, we can see the Lover coloring an essentially ascetic and moralistic religion with his irrepressible passion.

The love between the Father and the Son in the doctrine of the Trinity is often described in terms little short of libidinous. And the doctrine of the incarnation itself proclaims God's "historical" impregnation of a human woman and, through their union, God's permanent and intimate intercourse with all human beings. It is the presence of the Lover in Christian mystical experience and theological thought that underlies the Church's ambivalent, but nonetheless sacramental, view of the material universe.

But for all of this, the Christian church overall has remained hostile to the Lover. The Lover has fared little better in Judaism. In Orthodox Judaism, the Lover, projected onto women, is still depreciated. The traditional Jewish prayer books still include, as part of the preliminary morning service, the sentence "Blessed art thou, Lord our God, King of the universe, who hast not made me a woman." And in Judaism, so the story goes, Eve was the one who first sinned. This slander against women, and by implication, against the Lover with whom she has been linked, sets the stage for the Jewish (and later the Christian and Moslem) notion of the woman as "seductress" who works to distract pious men from their pursuit of "holiness."

In Islam women have been notoriously depreciated and oppressed. Islam is a religion of Warrior energy asceticism. But even here the Lover has not been banished. The Moslem paradise after death is shown as Lover territory. Here all that the Moslem saint has forsworn and repressed in his earthly life is restored to him in the form of an endless banquet at which he is attended by beautiful women, "black-eyed houris."

Hinduism is different; it is not a moralistic or ethical religion in the same sense that the Western religions are. Its spirituality is much more aesthetic and mystical. At the same time that Hinduism celebrates the Oneness of all things (in Brahman) and the human oneness with God (in Atman) it also rejoices in the world of forms and delights in the realm of the senses.

The Hindu worshiper has many gods and goddesses to experience, many exotic shapes and colors, half-animal and half-human, plants, and even stones, all of them the manifold and sensuously luxuriating forms of the One who stands behind them, pouring his infinite love and passion into them. Hinduism celebrates the erotic aspect of the Lover, divinely incarnated in the world in its sacred love poetry (the *Kama Sutra*, for instance) and in the arousing forms of some of its temple sculptures. If you think that the King/Warrior/Magician and the Lover are fundamentally opposed, a visit to the Hindu temple at Konarak will correct this impression. At Konarak, gods and goddesses, men and women, are shown luxuriating in every conceivable sexual position, in an ecstasy of union with each other, with the universe, and with God.

In this connection, a man in his early thirties, feeling stifled and sterile in both his work and his personal life, came in for analysis. He was an accountant, and he was feeling increasingly detached from his daily ciphering and figuring. He felt hemmed in by the codes of behavior that can be a part of any number of such "straight" professions, as he described them. He felt cut off from, as he said, "the muck and mire of real life." It became clear that he was not in touch with the Lover within.

Then he had a dream, which he called "The Dream of the Indian Girl." In the dream, he found himself in India, a place he had never thought much about before. He was walking through a rat-infested slum. What struck him first were the colors—blues, oranges, whites, reds, and maroons. Then it was the smells—exotic spices and perfumes along with the stench of human waste and decaying garbage. He climbed a rickety staircase to a second-floor apartment, and there he saw a dirty, but radiantly beautiful dusky Indian girl, dressed in rags. They made love on a stained and dirty mattress on the floor.

When he woke up, he felt a sense of excitement, refreshment, and joy he had never known before. He described his feeling as a kind of "spirituality." In the dream, he had felt the presence of "God" as an exotic, sensuous Being, one who enjoyed the love-making right along with him. This was a revelation to him, and he began to access, with great benefit to himself and his sexual partners, the mature masculine energies of the Lover.

What ways of life manifest the Lover most clearly? There are two primary ones—the artist (broadly defined) and the psychic. Painters, musicians, poets, sculptors, and writers are often "mainlining" the Lover. The artist is well known to be sensitive and sensual. To see this, we need only look at the light-charged figures of Gauguin, the flashing colors of the Impressionists, the nudes of Goya, the sculptures of Henry Moore. We need only hear the moody mysticism of Mahler's symphonies, the "cool" jazz of the group Hiroshima, or the sensuous, undulating poems of Wallace Stevens. Artists' personal lives are typically, perhaps stereotypically, stormy, messy, and labyrinthine—full of ups and downs, failed marriages, and often substance abuse. They live very close to the fiery power of the creative unconscious.

In a similar way, genuine psychics also live in a world of sensations and "vibrations," of deeply felt intuitions. Their conscious awareness, like that of the artist, is extraordinarily open to invasion from other people's thoughts and feelings and from the murky realm of the collective unconscious. They seem to move in a world behind or beneath the world of daylight common sense. From this hidden world they receive, often in the form of almost audible words, gusts of strong feelings, unaccounted-for smells, sensations of heat and cold not accessible to others, images of great horror and beauty, and clues about what is really going on with people. They may even receive impressions about the future. All those men who are successfully "reading" cards, tea leaves, and palms are accessing the Lover, who binds all things together under the surface, who even binds the future with the present.

The businessman who has "hunches" is also accessing the Lover. So are we all when we have premonitions and intuitions about people, situations, or our own future. In those moments, the underlying unity of things is revealed to us, even in mundane ways, and we are drawn into the Lover energy, which connects us with realities of which we are not normally aware.

Any artistic or creative endeavor and almost every profession, from farming to stockbroking, from house painting to computer software designing, is drawing upon the energies of the Lover for creativity.

So are connoisseurs, those men who really appreciate fine foods, wines, tobaccos, coins, primitive artifacts, and a host of other material objects. So are the so-called buffs. Steam train buffs have a sensuous, even erotic, affinity for these great, shining black "phalluses." The car-lover looking for just the right Corvette, the used-car appraiser who delights in touching and smelling the cars, in looking for the beauty and the defects beneath the rust and the soiled interiors, the "fan" of a particular literary genre or rock group—all these are accessing the Lover. The connoisseur of rich coffees, of chocolates; the antique dealer who cherishes a Ming vase, turning it over and over in his hands—the Lover is expressing himself through them all. The minister whose sermons are animated by images and stories, who is, as the Native Americans said, "thinking with his heart" instead of only with his head, is accessing the Lover. The Lover is singing through his sermons. All of us, when we stop doing and just let ourselves be and *feel* without the pressure to perform, when we "stop to smell the roses," are feeling the Lover.

Of course, we feel him strongly in our love lives. In our culture, this is the main avenue most of us have for getting in touch with the Lover. Many men literally live for the thrill of "falling in love"—that is, falling into the power of the Lover. In this ecstatic consciousness, which comes to even the most hard-boiled of us, we delight in our beloved and cherish her in all her beauty of body and soul. Through our emotional and physical union with her, we are transported into a Divine World of ecstasy and pleasure, on the one hand, and pain and sorrow, on the other. We join with the troubadours in exclaiming, "I know the pangs of love!" The whole world looks and feels different to us, more alive, more vivid, more meaningful, for better and for worse. This is the work of the Lover.

Before we move on to a discussion of the shadow side of the Lover, we want to take note of the old issue of monogamy versus polygamy and promiscuity. Monogamy arises out of the "amor" form of love, in which one man and one woman give themselves to each other alone—body and soul. It shows up in the mythological world in stories about the love between the Egyptian god Osiris and his wife, Isis, and the Canaanite god Baal's love for his wife, Anath.

In Hindu mythology, there is the undying love between Shiva and Parvati. And in the Bible we see the long-suffering love of Yahweh for Israel, his "bride." Monogamy is still our ideal today, at least in the West. But the Lover also expresses himself through polygamy, serial monogamy, or promiscuity. In mythology, this is shown in the Hindu Krishna's love for the *gopis*, the female cowherds. He loves each of them fully, with all his infinite capacity to love, so that each feels absolutely special and valued. In Greek mythology, Zeus has many beloveds, in both the divine and the human worlds. In human history, the Lover in this guise has manifested in the kingly harems, viewed from the monogamous perspective with such horror and, at the same time, such fascination. The Egyptian pharaoh Ramses II is believed to have had over one hundred wives, not to mention innumerable concubines. The biblical kings David and Solomon had large harems of delectable women, and, as we see in *The King and I*, so did the King of Siam. Some wealthy Moslem men to this day maintain a number of wives and concubines. The Lover manifests in all of these social arrangements.

The Shadow Lover: The Addicted and the Impotent Lover

A man living in either pole of the Lover's Shadow, like a man living in any of the shadow forms of the masculine energies, is *possessed* by the very energy that could be a source of life and well-being for him, if accessed appropriately. As long as he is possessed by the Shadow Lover, however, the energy works to his destruction and to the destruction of others around him.

The most forceful and urgent question a man identified with the *Addicted* Lover asks is: "Why should I put any limits on my sensual and sexual experience of this vast world, a world that holds unending pleasures for me?"

How does the Addict possess a man? The primary and most deeply disturbing characteristic of the Shadow Lover as Addict is his lostness, which shows up in a number of ways. A man possessed by the Shadow Lover becomes literally lost in an ocean of the senses, not just "in sunsets," or "in reverie." The slightest impressions from the outer world are enough to pull him off center. He gets drawn into the loneliness of a train whistle in the night, into the emotional devastation of a fight at the office, into the blandishments of the women he encounters on the street. Pulled first one way and then another, he is not the master of his own fate. He becomes the victim of his own sensitivity. He becomes enmeshed in the world of sights, sounds, smells, and tactile sensations. We can think here of the painter Van Gogh, who got lost in his paint and canvases and in the violent dynamism of the nighttime stars he depicted.

There is the case of an excruciatingly sensitive man who could not tolerate the least bit of light in his room at night, who went literally crazy because of noises from the other apartments in his building, and who, at the same time, was a brilliant would-be composer. He couldn't keep melodies and lyrics from running through his thoughts. He heard them audibly. In a desperate attempt to keep his life minimally structured, he wrote hundreds of memoranda to himself and stuck them up all around his apartment—on the mirrors, over his bed, on the coffee table, on the door frames. In a frenzy, he ran from one note to another, trying frantically to meet every obligation. His life was a chaos of oversensitivity. He was lost in his own senses.

Another man was studying Hebrew at night school. Possessed by the Addicted Lover, he approached the language sensuously, delighting in every one of the strange characters and feeling profoundly every sound and the subtle nuances of the words. Eventually, he reached a point at which he was totally absorbed by his feelings, and he couldn't continue to learn. He couldn't achieve the detachment necessary to memorize. He lost the energy to take in even one more word. And though he had started at the top of his class, he soon fell to the bottom.

He was not controlling and mastering the language; it was controlling him. He became an addict to Hebrew, a victim of the feelings he found in it. He became lost.

One man had a love for vintage cars that exceeded his income. He was lured on and on—"lost" in their glistening beauty, oblivious to the drain on his finances until the day "harsh reality" came knocking, and he discovered he was bankrupt. Then he had to sell his beloved cars just to keep himself afloat.

There is a story of an artist who took the last money in the house, the money his wife needed to buy their two babies formula for the next week, and spent it on grease pencils and pastels for the art project he was working on. He loved his wife and children. But, as he said, he felt absolutely compelled to express his art. He got lost in it; finally, he lost his family.

There are stories of so-called addictive personalities—people who can't stop eating, or drinking, or smoking, or using drugs. A young man who was a heavy cigarette smoker was warned by his doctor to quit or he was liable to get lung cancer. (He was showing the preliminary warning signs.) Though he wanted to live, he simply could not quit; he enjoyed the sensual satisfaction of the cigarettes so much. He did die, smoking to the end, lost in the chemical and emotional addiction of tobacco.

This lostness shows up, too, in the way that the Addict lives for the pleasure of the moment only and locks us into a web of immobility from which we cannot escape. This is what the theologian Reinhold Niebuhr talked about as "the sin of sensuality." And it's what the Hindus talk about as *maya*—the dance of illusion, the intoxicating (addictive) dance of sensuous things that enchants and enthralls the mind, catching us up in the cycles of pleasure and pain.

What happens when we are caught in the fires of love, roasting in the agony and the ecstasy of our own longings, is that we are unable to disincarnate, to step back, to act. We are unable to, as we say, "come to ourselves." We are unable to detach and to gain distance from our feelings. Many are the lives that are ruined because people cannot extricate themselves from destructive marriages and relationships. Whenever we

Don Juan (Courtesy of The Bettman Archive.)

feel ourselves caught in an addictive relationship, we had better beware, because the chances are very good that we have become victims of the Shadow Lover.

In his lostness—within and without—the victim of the active pole of the Shadow Lover is eternally restless. This is the man who is always searching for something. He doesn't know what it is he's looking for, but he's the cowboy at the end of the movie riding off alone into the sunset seeking some other excitement, some other adventure, unable to settle down. He has an insatiable hunger to experience some vague something that is just over the next hill. He is compelled to extend the frontiers not of knowledge (for that would be liberating for him) but of his sensuality, no matter what the cost to the mortal man who badly needs, as all mortal men do, merely human happiness. This is James Bond and Indiana Jones, loving and leaving to love again, and leave again.

Here's where we see the Don Juan syndrome, and where we can touch base with the monogamy/promiscuity issue again. Monogamy (though not in a simple way) can be seen as the product of a man's own deep rootedness and centeredness. He is bounded, not by external rules but by his own inner structures, his own sense of his masculine well-being and calm, and his own inner joy. But the man moving from one woman to another, compulsively searching for he knows not what, is a man whose inner structures have not yet solidified. Because he himself is fragmented within, and not centered, he is pushed and pulled around by the illusory wholeness he thinks is out there in the world of feminine forms and sensual experiences.

For the Addict, the world presents itself as tantalizing fragments of a lost whole. Caught in the foreground, he can't see the underlying background. Caught in the "myriads of forms," as the Hindus say, he can't find the Oneness that would bring him calm and stability. Living on the finite side of the prism, he can only experience light in its dazzling but fractured rainbow hues.

This is another way of talking about what ancient religions called idolatry. The addicted Lover unconsciously invests the finite fragments of his experience with the power of the Unity, which he can never experience. This shows up, again, in the interesting phenomenon of pornography collections. Men under the fragmenting energy of the Addict will often amass huge collections of photographs of nude women and then arrange them in categories like "breasts," "legs," and so on. Then, they will lay the "breasts" out side-by-side and delight in comparing them. And they will do the same with "legs" and other bits and pieces of the female anatomy. They marvel at the beauty of the parts, but they can't experience a woman as a whole being physically or psychologically, and certainly not as a unity of body and soul, a complete person with whom they could have an intimate, human relationship.

There is an unconscious inflation in this idolatry, for the mortal man in this frame of mind is experiencing these images in the infinite sensuality of the God who made them in all their variety, and who delights in the fragments of his creation as well as in the whole. This man, captured by the Addicted Lover, is unconsciously identifying himself with God as Lover.

The restlessness of the man under the power of the Addict is an expression of his search for a way out of the spider's web. The man who is possessed by the web of maya is twisting and turning, frantically struggling to find a way out of the world. "Stop the world. I want to get off!" But instead of taking the only way out there is, he struggles and deepens his predicament. He is thrashing in quicksand and just sinking deeper.

This happens because what he thinks is the way out is really the way deeper in. What the Addict is seeking (though he doesn't know it) is the ultimate and continuous "orgasm," the ultimate and continuous "high." This is why he rides from village to village and from adventure to adventure. This is why he goes from one woman to another. Each time his woman confronts him with her mortality, her finitude, her weakness and limitations, hence shattering his dream of *this time* finding the orgasm without end—in other words, when the excitement of the illusion of perfect union with her (with the world, with God) becomes tarnished—he saddles his horse and rides out looking for renewal of his ecstasy. He needs his "fix" of masculine joy. He really does. He just doesn't know where to look for it. He ends by looking for his "spirituality" in a line of cocaine.

Psychologists talk about the problems that stem from a man's possession by the Addict as "boundary issues." For the man possessed by the Addict, there are no boundaries. As we've said, the Lover does not want to be limited. And, when we are possessed by him, we cannot *stand* to be limited.

A man possessed by the Addicted Lover is really a man possessed by the unconscious—his own personal unconscious and the collective unconscious. He is overwhelmed by it as if by the sea. One man dreamed repeatedly of running through the streets of Chicago, hiding behind the skyscrapers from a huge, miles-high wave from Lake Michigan that was racing shoreward and threatening to inundate the Sear's Tower. His sleep was disturbed every night, not only by this dream, but also by a "flood" of dreams. He had, as it turned out, insufficient boundaries between his conscious Ego and the overpowering force of the unconscious.

The fact that the unconscious appeared to him as a tidal wave from the lake (recall the sorcerer's apprentice!) is very much in keeping with the universal image of the unconscious as the chaotic "deep" of the Bible, as the primeval ocean of the ancient creation myths from which the masculine world of structure emerged. This oceanic chaos—the unconscious—is, as we have seen, imaged in many mythologies as feminine. It is Mother, and it represents the Baby Boy's claustrophobic sense of merger with her. The tidal wave dreamer was, in reality, being threatened by the overwhelming force of his unresolved Mother issues. What he needed to do was develop his masculine Ego structures outside the "feminine" unconscious. He needed to go back to the Hero stage of masculine development and slay the dragon of his overconnectedness with his mortal mother and with the Mother—the "God, All-Mother, Mighty."

This is exactly what the Addict prevents us from doing. It stands opposed to boundaries. But boundaries, constructed with heroic effort, are what a man possessed by the Addict needs most. He doesn't need more oneness with all things. He's already got too much of that. What he needs is distance and detachment.

We can see, then, how the Shadow Lover as Addict is a carryover from childhood into adulthood of the absorption into the Mother of the Mama's Boy. The man under the power of the Addict is still within the Mother, and he's struggling to get out. There's a fascinating scene in the movie *Mishima* in which the young Mishima is tantalized to the point of obsession with the image of a Golden Temple (the Mother, the unconscious). It is so beautiful to him that it is painful. It becomes so painful that in order to break free of it he must burn it. He must destroy the alluring and enchanting "feminine" beauty that would keep him from his manhood. And he does so.

This need to detach from and to contain the chaotic power of the "feminine" unconscious may also go a long way toward accounting for our masculine sexual perversions, especially those perversions that show up in "bondage" and in the violent sexual humiliation of women. We can see these repulsive acts as attempts, like Mishima's, to "tie down," to repudiate in order to disempower the overwhelming power of the unconscious in our lives.

If the Mama's Boy's desire is to touch what it is forbidden to touch—that is, the Mother—and to cross boundaries that he regards as being artificial—ultimately, the incest taboo—the Addict, arising as he does out of the Mama's Boy, must learn about the usefulness of boundaries the hard way. He must learn that his lack of masculine structure, his lack of discipline, his resulting affairs, and his authority problems will inevitably get him into trouble. He will be fired from his jobs, and his wife, who loves him dearly, will eventually leave him.

What happens if we feel that we are out of touch with the Lover in his fullness? We are then possessed by the Impotent Lover. We will experience our lives in an unfeeling way. We will "feel" the sterility and flatness the accountant reported. We will describe symptoms that psychologists call "flattened affect"—lack of enthusiasm, lack of vividness, lack of aliveness. We will feel bored and listless. We may have trouble getting up in the morning and trouble going to sleep at night. We may find ourselves speaking in a monotone. We may find ourselves increasingly alienated from our family, our co-workers, and our friends. We may feel hungry but lack an appetite. Everything may begin to feel like the passage in the biblical book of Ecclesiastes that declares, "All is vanity, and a striving after wind," and, "There is nothing new under the sun." In short, we will become depressed.

People who are habitually possessed by the Impotent Lover are *chronically* depressed. They feel a lack of connection with others, and they feel cut off from themselves. We see this in therapy often. The therapist will be able to tell from the expression on the client's face or from his body language that some feeling is trying to express itself. But if we ask the client what he is feeling, he will have absolutely no idea. He may say something like, "I don't know. I just feel there's this kind of fog. Everything is just hazy." This often happens when the client is getting too close to really "hot" material. What happens then is that a shield goes up between the conscious Ego and the feeling. That shield is depression.

This disconnection can reach serious proportions known to psychology as "dissociative phenomena," a condition in which (among other things) the client may start speaking about himself in the third person. Instead of saying, "I feel" this or that, he will say, "John feels this." He may have a sense of himself as unreal. His life may seem like a movie that he is watching. These men are seriously, and dangerously, possessed by the Impotent Lover.

But we all know that when we're depressed that we just don't have the motivation to do the things we either want to do or have to do. This frequently happens to the elderly. Their physical problems, isolation, and lack of useful work plunge them into depression. The zest for life is gone. The Lover seems nowhere to be found. Pretty soon these older men stop fixing meals for themselves. They feel that there is nothing to live for. The Bible says that "without a vision, the people perish." It is specifically without the imaging and visioning of the Lover that people perish.

But it isn't just the lack of a vision that signifies the oppressive power of the Impotent Lover in a man's life. It is also the absence of an erect and eager penis. This man's sex life has gone stale; he is sexually inactive. Such sexual inactivity may stem from any number of factors—boredom and lack of ecstasy with his mate, smoldering anger about his relationship, tension and stress on the job, money worries, or the sense of being emasculated by the feminine or by the other men in his life. In conjunction with the Impotent Lover, this man is either regressed into a presexual Boy or he is mainlining either the Warrior or the Magician, or a combination of the three. His sexual and sensual sensitivity has been overwhelmed by other concerns. As his sexual partner becomes more demanding, he withdraws even further into the passive pole of the Lover's Shadow. At this point, the opposite pole of the archetypal Shadow may "rescue" him by propelling him into the Addict's quest for the perfect satisfaction of his sexuality beyond the mundane world of his primary relationship.

Accessing the Lover

If we are appropriately accessing the Lover, but keeping our Ego structures strong, we feel related, connected, alive, enthusiastic, compassionate, empathic, energized, and romantic about our lives, our goals, our work, and our achievements. It is the Lover, properly accessed, that gives us a sense of meaning—what we have been calling spirituality. It is the Lover who is the source of our longings for a better world for ourselves and others. He it is who is the idealist, and the dreamer. He is the one who wants us to have an abundance of good things. "I have come to bring you life, that you might have it more abundantly," says the Lover.

The Lover keeps the other masculine energies humane, loving, and related to each other and to the real life situation of human beings struggling in a difficult world. The King, the Warrior, and the Magician, as we've suggested, harmonize pretty well with each other. They do so because, without the Lover, they are all essentially detached from life. They need the Lover to energize them, to humanize them, and to give them their ultimate purpose—love. They need the Lover to keep them from becoming sadistic.

The Lover needs them as well. The Lover without boundaries, in his chaos of feeling and sensuality, needs the King to define limits for him, to give him structure, to order his chaos so that it can be channeled creatively. Without limits, the Lover energy turns negative and destructive. The Lover needs the Warrior in order to be able to act decisively, in order to detach, with the clean cut of the sword, from the web of immobilizing sensuality. The Lover needs the Warrior to destroy the Golden Temple, which keeps him fixated. And the Lover needs the

Magician to help him back off from the ensnaring effect of his emotions, in order to reflect, to get a more objective perspective on things, to disconnect—enough at least to see the big picture and to experience the reality beneath the seeming.

Tragically, the unrelenting attacks on our vitality and on our "shining" begin early in our lives. Many of us may have so repressed the Lover in us that it has become very hard for us to feel passionate about anything in our lives. The trouble with most of us is not that we feel too much passion, but that we don't feel our passion much at all. We don't feel our joy. We don't feel able to be alive and to live our lives the way we wanted to live them when we began. We may even think that feelings and, in particular, *our* feelings, are annoying encumbrances and inappropriate for a man. But let us not surrender our lives! Let us find the spontaneity and joy of life inside ourselves. Then not only will we live our lives more abundantly, but we will enable others to live, perhaps for the first time in *their* lives.

Conclusion:

Accessing the Archetypal Powers of the Mature Masculine

When *Lord of the Flies,* William Golding's classic novel about English schoolboys marooned on a tropical island, was recently redone in cinematic form, critics of the new movie asked why the story had been remade. Even though this latest film version of Golding's story may not be the best cinema, the answer is that this work, in whatever form, speaks directly and powerfully about the human situation on this planet.

It may be that there never has been a time when the archetypes of the mature masculine (or the mature feminine) were dominant in human life. It seems that we as a species live under the curse of infantilism—and maybe always have. Thus, patriarchy is really "puer-archy" (i.e., the rule of boys), and perhaps our human world has always rather resembled Golding's island. But at least there used to be structures and systems—rituals—for evoking a greater level of masculine maturity than seems to be the rule in our antisystem, antiritual, antisymbol world today. At least there were at one time sacred kings, upon whom the men in the realm could project their inner King and thus activate this masculine energy form indirectly in themselves. Certainly, for both good and ill, there was a time when the Warrior energy was active and effective in shaping the lives of men and the civilizations they built. And, though always the prerogative of only a few, the Magician was available to help individual men with their life problems and to gain for the society some control over the unpredictable world of nature. And the Lover was also held in high regard in the cultures that celebrated seers and prophets, cave painters and poets.

All that is changed now, cashed in for personal wealth and self-aggrandizement, the currency of the day. Yet ours is a world that needs the masculine energies in their maturity more urgently than ever before in human history. It is a strange irony that at the very moment when all of civilization seems to be nearing its greatest initiation ever—from a fragmented, tribal way of life to a more whole, more universal life—that just at this moment, the ritual processes for turning boys into men have all but disappeared from the planet. Just at the time when it is necessary for survival that immaturity be replaced by maturity—that boys become men and girls become women, and that grandiosity be replaced by true greatness—we are thrown back upon our own inner resources as men, struggling toward a wiser future for ourselves and our world pretty much alone. Maybe this is as it should be. The evolutionary process has placed the powerful resources of the four masculine archetypes within every man and has called upon them in different periods of human history to solve difficult problems and to dare the unthinkable—to organize laws out of chaos, to stimulate enormous outpourings of creativity and generativity (like those that produced early civilizations), to gain some capacity to steward nature, both inner and outer, and to arouse tender appreciation and relatedness. Perhaps this growth process of our species has also arranged for the radical internalizing and psychologizing of these forces in modern men.

If ours is an age of individualism in the deepest as well as in the most shallow sense, then let us be individuals! Let us nurture and welcome great individuals—individual men who will, with the benevolence of ancient kings, the courage and decisiveness of ancient warriors, the wisdom of magicians, and the passion of lovers, move energetically to take up the challenge of saving a world that has been cast down before us. There are certainly global needs and work enough to keep every man busy for the foreseeable future.

Our effectiveness in meeting these challenges is directly related to how we as individual men meet the challenges of our own immaturity. How well we transform ourselves from men living our lives under the power of Boy psychology to real men guided by the archetypes of Man psychology will have a decisive effect on the outcome of our present world situation.

Techniques

We have briefly sketched the dimensions of the problem in this short book. We have delineated the immature and the mature energy forms. We have shown something about how they interact with each other and how they give rise to each other, in their shadow forms and in their fullness. We have touched on some techniques for accessing them. In the pages remaining, we look more closely at some of these techniques for reconnecting appropriately with the archetypes of masculine maturity.

The first step in doing this, for each of us, is critical self-appraisal. We have said that there is no use asking ourselves *if* the negative or shadow sides of the archetypes are showing up in our lives. The realistic, honest question we need to ask is *how* they are manifesting. Let us remember that the key to maturity, to moving from Boy psychology to Man psychology, is to become humble, to be grasped by humility. Humility is not humiliation. We're not asking any man to submit himself to humiliation at his own or others' hands. Far from it! But we all need to be humble. Let us recall that true humility consists of two things: the first is knowing our limitations, and the second is getting the help we need.

Assuming that we all could use some help, we now look at three important techniques for accessing the positive resources we are missing in our lives.

Active Imagination Dialogue

In the first of these techniques, called in psychology active imagination dialogue, the conscious Ego enters into dialogue with various unconscious entities, other focused consciousnesses, other points of view, within us. Behind these different points of view, sometimes in obscure ways, lie the archetypes—in both their positive and their negative forms. We all dialogue with ourselves anyway, but usually inefficiently, when we "talk to ourselves." It's a joke, of course, that says, "It's OK to talk to yourself, as long as you don't answer." But we *do* answer ourselves. And we do it all the time. We answer ourselves sometimes verbally, out loud, or in our heads. Often, though, we answer ourselves through the events and people that "happen" into our lives without our conscious willing or intention. We answer ourselves too by acting out a point of view or an attitude that we consciously abhor.

Every man has had the experience, for example, of planning what to say and do before he enters a high-level meeting or goes off to yell at the repair shop for incompetent work, and then doing and saying something else. In the meeting, he had planned to keep his cool and calmly and firmly set out his point of view. But when others started getting upset, he suddenly found himself angrily trying to outshout his opponents. At the garage his planned tirade was cut short by an unexpectedly sympathetic-sounding desk clerk, and he ended by being congenial, when he knew well enough that the guy was just soft-soaping him. Two thousand years ago, Paul, in great frustration, asked himself the question, "Why do I do the things I don't want to do; and the very things I want to do, I can't?" And, when the scene, whatever it is, is over, we say to ourselves, "I don't know what came over me!"

What came over us, what changed our planned words and behaviors, is what psychology calls an autonomous complex, and behind it what we are calling a pole in a bipolar archetypal Shadow. It pays to face these rebellious and often negative energy forms before they make us say and do things we regret.

Active imagination dialogue is one important technique for actually holding conversations, board meetings, conference calls with these energy forms that wear our faces but are timeless and universal. In active imagination dialogue we talk with them, contacting one or more of them and giving our point of view. Then we listen for their replies. Often, it is best to do this on paper, writing both the Ego's thoughts and feelings and the "opponent's" thoughts and feelings just as they come, without censoring them. As in any successful board meeting, we at least need to agree to disagree. Under extremely hostile circumstances, we need to reach a simple truce, if possible, at least for the time being. At a minimum, this kind of exercise will help us to scope out the opposition and get most of the cards on the table. Forewarned is forearmed.

This exercise may seem strange at first. But usually just a few moments of writing will reveal the reality of the other points of view within every man's psyche. It may happen that you draw a blank at first. But if you persist in talking to yourself, eventually you will be answered. The answers you get may be startling. They may be reassuring. But they will come.

One word of caution: if in the course of this exercise you encounter a really hostile presence, what some psychologists call an inner persecutor, stop the exercise and consult a good therapist. Most of us probably have inner persecutors, as well as inner helpers. But the persecutor may be so vicious that you will need support to continue dialoguing with it. If you suspect you will run into one of these, it is best to invoke a positive archetypal energy form before you even open the dialogue. (We talk about invocation in the next section.) One more note: you may get in touch with more than one other point of view. Treat the dialogue, then, as a board meeting, and listen to what everybody has to say.

What follows is an example of an active imagination dialogue exercise. The man who had this dialogue with one of his complexes (the Trickster) had been having a lot of trouble at work because he found himself unable to contain his critical comments—most of which were based on accurate observations—about management's incompetence. He found himself ridiculing his boss in front of his fellow employees; he was unable to make it to work on time, and was unable to contain his restlessness and disgust in meetings, occasionally in direct one-on-one confrontations with his supervisor. The following is what happened when he sat down to try to get in touch with whatever was causing him to behave this way. (E stands for Ego, and T stands for Trickster.)

E: Who are you? [*Pause*] Who are you? [*Pause*] What do you want? [*Long pause*] Whoever you are, you're getting me in trouble.

T: Isn't that interesting?

E: Oh, so there *is* someone there.

T: Don't be a smart ass. Of course there's someone here. I wish I could say the same for you. The lights are on, but nobody's home!

E: What do you want with me?

T: Well, let me think about it. [*Pause*] You know what I want, you idiot. I want to make your life miserable.

E: Why?

T: Why? [*mockingly*] Because it's fun. You think you're so cool. Just imagine if you got fired! Boy, that would be fun!

E: Who are you?

T: My name isn't important. What's important is that I'm here.

E: Why do you want to make my life miserable? Why is that fun for you?

T: Because you deserve a miserable life. *I'm* miserable.

E: Why are you miserable?

T: Because of what you've done to me.

E: *Me* done to *you*?!

T: Yeah, you jerk.

E: What have I done to you?

T: You don't care about me, so don't pretend that you do.

E: I do care. I want to care.

T: Yeah, because you're uncomfortable.

E: That's right. You and I have to settle things between us.

T: No, we don't. You just have to get fired.

E: I won't let you get me fired.

T: Just try to stop me!

After more mutual accusation and expressions of distrust, the man's

Ego and this inner figure, which was the Trickster archetype wearing the man's own personal shadow identity, began serious conversation.

T: You put down your real feelings about things—all of your feelings. You're a wimp. I *am* your feelings, your *real* feelings. I want to be angry sometimes, and I want to be really glad! And you just wimp around, acting superior. Any superiority you have is in me. I'm the real you!

E: I want to be your friend. And . . . I need you to be mine. You are not me. I have my own point of view, and I need you to hear it. But I really will turn over a new leaf. At the same time, I can't let you just blurt things out at work. If I go hungry, so do you. We're in this together, you know.

T: Yeah, OK. But you're going to have to pay attention to me. We've got vacation time coming up, and I want to go someplace this year. Wine, women, song! So, you're going to have to buy some clothes, and a ticket to someplace—I'd like the tropics! And, what's more—and don't be shocked—I want to get laid!

E: It's a deal. And you take the pressure off of me at work, or we'll be on *permanent* vacation.

T: That was the idea. I was going to force you to take a vacation of *some* kind. Just don't back out on our deal.

E: I won't.

T: Then it's a deal.

Often, conducting a dialogue with inner "opponents"—usually forms of the immature masculine energies—will defuse much of their power. What they—like all children—really want is to be noticed, honored, and taken seriously. And they have a right to be. Once they are honored, and their feelings validated, they no longer need to act out through our lives.

This conflict ended amicably. And what had been a nonrelationship became a new source of balance in this man's life. His Trickster had finally deflated him—and had done so in order to force him to fulfill aspects of his personality that he had ignored. A figure who started out as an inner persecutor became a lifelong friend.

In this next example of active imagination dialogue, the man's Ego acted as a referee for two conflicting aspects of his personality, one showing the influence of the immature Hero energy and the other the Lover. The two archetypes were in conflict about how to treat the woman in the man's life. The Hero wanted to conquer her, while the Lover wanted to just relate to her on a mutual basis. This is how the dialogue went. (E stands for Ego, H for Hero, and L for Lover.)

E: All right, you two. We've got a problem. Gail wants to go to Brazil on a lark—without us. You—Hero—want to blast her for it and deliver an ultimatum: either drop the trip and come to Chicago to visit you instead, or forget the relationship. And you—Lover—just want to let her go and love her no matter what. So, we have to decide something here.

H: She's being selfish! As usual, she's trying to overwhelm me with her impulsive desires. She doesn't care about me. She's dangerous. And if I'm going to be in a relationship with her, I'm going to have to lay down the law.

L: Yes, but that takes all the fun out of it. She has to *want* to be with us, or it's no good. I'll love her no matter what she does. I'm so in love with her; if you try to control her, you'll ruin what real love is.

H: Don't give me that romantic crap! Maybe you want to lie down and take this, but I can't! How can you even think about living with such a selfish and impulsive woman?

L: Because, selfish and impulsive or not, she's the woman I love.

H: But there's no kind of security with this woman!

L: There's also no security in forcing someone to do what you want against their own wishes. Love loves just for the pure joy of loving.

H: Well, maybe you can live with pure joy, but I can't. I will defeat her willfulness or die trying.

L: What will die is the relationship!

E: OK. You've each presented your point of view. Now, we've got to come to some kind of agreement. It seems to me you're both right, but both excessive. The Hero is right in setting reasonable limits on the relationship, and in recognizing our own limits, what we are comfortable with. Gail's going to Brazil instead of coming to Chicago is beyond endurance. And the Lover is right in not wanting to blow off the relationship, and in wanting to respect *Gail's* limits and *her* desires. But, Lover, you have to realize that human love *does* have limits. It is not limitless. Oh, the love may be. But what we can *live with* is not. So, let's both set limits and love Gail at the same time.

Because the Hero, under the influence of the Lover, was able to transform his fear and anger into courage and limit-setting—something Gail was actually looking for—Gail did not go to Brazil and is maturing in the relationship. And the split psyche of the man is becoming integrated.

Invocation

A second technique we call invocation. This time we access the masculine archetypes in their fullness as positive energy forms. This too may seem strange at first. But a moment's reflection will reveal to us that we do this kind of thing all the time. We all live our psychological lives unintentionally, for the most part, invoking images and thoughts that may or may not be helpful to us. Our minds are cluttered with sights, sounds, and words, many of which are unwanted. To see the truth of this, just close your eyes for a moment. Images will present themselves in the darkness, and thoughts, barely audible to the inner "ear," will crowd into your mind. If active imagination dialogue is a conscious, focused way of talking to yourself, invocation is a conscious, focused way of calling up the images you *want* to see. Imaging deeply affects our moods, our attitudes, the way we look at things, and what we do.

It is therefore important what thoughts and images we are invoking in our lives. Here's how to do focused imaging, or invocation:

If possible, find a quiet place and time, clear your mind as best you can and relax—again, as best you can. (We don't recommend long relaxation exercises as a necessary part of this process, although they can be helpful.) Focus on an image that has both mental pictures and spoken words (spoken in your head, at least). It is often useful to spend some time looking for images of the King, the Warrior, the Magician, the Lover. Use those images in your invocations. Let's say you've found an image of a Roman emperor on his throne—a still from a movie, perhaps, or a painting. During this exercise, set that image in front of you. As you relax, talk to the image. Call up the King inside yourself. Seek to merge your deep unconscious with him. Realize that you (as an Ego) are different from him. In your imagination, make your Ego his servant. Feel his calm and his strength, his balanced benevolence toward you, his watching over you. Imagine yourself before his throne, having an audience with him. In effect, "pray" to him. Tell him that you need him, that you need his help—his power, his favor, his orderliness, his manliness. Count on his generosity and his kind disposition.

A young man once entered therapy feeling very out of touch with his erotic side. He just couldn't make a "chemical" connection with women. He wanted more than anything else to find a woman who would love him, a woman with whom he could have an exciting sex life, a woman he could marry. Part of the prescription in his therapy was to read all he could about the Greek god of Love, Eros, especially the Cupid (Eros) and Psyche story, and then to pray to Eros to help him to feel sensual and attractive. Shortly after he began his invocations of this image of the Lover, he went on a cruise. There he met, quite unexpectedly, a beautiful woman who felt that he was the most handsome, manly man she'd ever seen. She was experiencing the newfound Eros within him, which was filling his whole personality with its force and radiance. She even said to him, "You're as handsome as a god!" Several nights out, they made passionate love in the sea, the most wonderful sexual experience of his life. The two stayed in touch with each other after the cruise, and within a year they were married, with a baby on the way. He attributed his new, more rewarding life to his imaging of and invocations to the Lover.

Another man found himself needled and attacked by several female co-workers for his self-confident, manly ways. He found strength in a crystal pyramid that he kept on his desk. (The pyramid form, as we have seen, is a symbol for the masculine Self.) Whenever he felt over-whelmed, he would take a sixty-second breather. He would turn to his pyramid and imagine it inside himself, in his chest. The waves of the emotional attacks on his manhood crashed against its sides, trying to fragment it. But the waves always fell back, eventually spending their fury. His work situation didn't improve, but he was able to keep his bal-ance, his calmness, and his centeredness most of the time, while he sought a better work environment. In the midst of a hectic day, this man could not fully ritualize his invocation. But many men, in the soli-tude of the late evening or the early morning, can. They sometimes even light candles and burn incense before an image of the archetype, honoring the archetype they are calling upon in an ancient, yet very appropriate, way.

What we are suggesting is comparable to what religions have always called prayer, when that prayer was accompanied by ritual accessing of the god. Far from being idols, icons in Greek Orthodoxy and statues in Roman Catholicism serve to focus an image of the energy form that the believer is invoking. The image of the saint or God may become so fixed in a man's mind that he no longer has to have a graphic representation in front of him to feel the energies that flow from it.

Admiring Men

Along the same lines is the related technique of admiration. Mature men need to admire other men, living and dead. We need especially to have contact with older men whom we can look up to. If such men are not available to us personally, we need to read their biographies and become familiar with their words and deeds. These men need not be perfect, because perfection—the realization of the completely whole man—can never be achieved. Movement toward wholeness is possible, however, and every man is individually responsible for it. It is precisely at our weak points, at those places within our psyches where we are possessed by the poles of an archetypal shadow system that we need to invoke, through active admiration, the strengths we lack but can appreciate in others. If we need more of the Warrior in our lives, we may come to know and appreciate the Warrior soul of the Egyptian pharaoh Ramses II, of the Zulu chief who threw himself and his men so courageously against the British in the nineteenth-century Zulu uprising, or of George Patton. If we need to more adequately access the King energy, we might study the life of Abraham Lincoln or Ho Chi Minh. If we need more Lover, we might admire the Lover energy of Leo Buscaglia.

The point is that what images and thoughts we invoke determine to a large extent not only how things *look* to us but how they actually *are*. A shift in our inner accessing of the archetypes of the mature masculine will effect a change in the outer circumstances and opportunities of our lives. At the very least, a changed inner world will greatly enhance our capacity to deal with difficult circumstances and eventually turn them to better advantage—for us, for those we love, and for our companies, our causes, and the world.

There's a saying in this connection: "Be careful what you wish for; you may get it!" The much-touted power of positive thinking is at least partially true, truer than most of us think. So while we are critically evaluating where we stand in relationship to the masculine energies, and while we are engaged in a dialogue with both positive and shadow aspects of them, we need also to be invoking the archetypes in their fullness in deliberate and focused ways.

Acting "As If"

There is yet another technique for accessing the archetypes of the mature masculine that deserves brief mention because it is so obvious it may get overlooked. It relies on the time-validated technology of the actor trying to "get into character" when he doesn't *feel* the character. This technique is called method acting. In this process, if you can't feel the character portrayed in your script, you begin by *acting like* the character. You move and talk as this character would move and talk.

You act "as if." On the stage, you act kingly, even if you've just been fired from your job and your wife has left you! "The show must go on," and others are depending on you to play your part well. So you pick up your script; you read the king's lines; you sit on the throne; and you *act like the king*. Pretty soon, believe it or not, you will start to feel like a king.

It's quite odd, but if you need to access more of the Lover, for example, and sunsets don't interest you, go out and really *look* at a sunset. Act *as if* you appreciate it. Notice the colors. Force yourself to see the beauty. Even say to yourself, "Oh, yes, look at those oranges and reds, and the subtle transition from blue to purple." Pretty soon, strange as it may seem, you really may find yourself becoming interested in the sunset!

If you need to access more of the Warrior, you might start by getting up from the television set some evening and forcing yourself out the door for a vigorous walk. You might take up a martial art. You might start an exercise class. You might force yourself to start on the unpaid bills piled on your desk. Get up. Move around! Start some action. And soon, much to your amazement, you may find yourself acting more like a Warrior in *many* areas of your life.

If you need to access the Magician more consciously, the next time someone comes to you for your wisdom, act as if you really have some. Act *as if* you really do have something helpful and insightful to say. Force yourself to really listen to this person. Try to clear your mind of your own agenda and really focus on the problem he or she is presenting to you. Then, as thoughtfully as you can, give that person as much of your accumulated life's wisdom as you can. We all have much more of this than we think we do.

A Final Word

In this book we have been concerned about helping men to take responsibility for the destructiveness of immature forms of masculinity. At the same time, it is clear that the world is overpopulated with not only immature men but also tyrannical and abusive little girls pretending to be women. It is time for men—particularly the men of Western civilization—to stop accepting the blame for everything that is wrong in the world. There has been a veritable blitzkrieg on the male gender, what amounts to an outright demonization of men and a slander against masculinity. But women are no more inherently responsible or mature than men are. The High Chair Tyrant, for instance, appears in all her or his splendor in both sexes. Men should never feel apologetic about their gender, as gender. They should be concerned with the maturation and the stewardship *of* that gender and of the larger world. The enemy for both sexes is not the other sex but infantile grandiosity and the splitting of the Self that results from it.

A final word of encouragement: any transformative process, like life itself, takes time and effort. We do our "homework" from the conscious side, and the unconscious, with its powerful resources, will, if approached in the right way, respond to our questions, our needs, and our woundedness in healing and generative ways. The struggle for maturity is a psychological, moral, and spiritual imperative from the Chinese Emperor within every man.

Joseph Campbell, in his last book, *The Inner Reaches of Outer Space*, called for a worldwide awakening to a kind of initiation that would become a rallying point for a deepened human sense of responsibility and maturity. Initiation, as we talk about it, is really a matter of exploring the *outer* reaches of *inner* space. We wish to add our voices to those of the many men throughout history who, against enormous odds, through their lives and through their teachings, have called for an end to the reign of the Lord of the Flies—the apocalyptic fantasy of the end of the world in a final display of infantile rage. If contemporary men can take the task of their own initiation from Boyhood to Manhood as seriously as did their tribal forebears, then we may witness the *end* of the *beginning* of our species, instead of the *beginning* of the *end*. We may pass between the clashing Scylla and Charybdis of our grandiosity and our chauvinistic tribalism and move beyond them into a future as wonderful and as generative as any depicted in the myths and legends that the King, the Warrior, the Magician, and the Lover have bequeathed to us.

Selected Readings

Ethology/Anthropology

Ardrey, Robert. *African Genesis.* New York: Dell, 1961.
———. *The Territorial Imperative.* New York: Dell, 1966.
Gilmore, David D. *Manhood in the Making: Cultural Concepts of Masculinity.* New Haven, CT: Yale Univ. Press, 1990.
Goodall, Jane. *The Chimpanzees of Gombe.* Cambridge, MA: Harvard Univ. Press, 1986.
Turner, Victor. *The Ritual Process.* Ithaca, NY: Cornell Univ. Press, 1969.

Comparative Mythology and Religion

Eliade, Mircea. *Cosmos and History.* New York: Harper & Row, 1959.
———. *Patterns in Comparative Religion.* Cleveland, OH: The World Publishing Co., 1963.
———. *The Sacred and the Profane.* New York: Harcourt, Brace & World, 1959.
Frazer, James G. *The Golden Bough.* New York: Macmillan, 1963.

Jung

Campbell, Joseph, ed. *The Portable Jung.* New York: Viking, 1971.
Edinger, Edward F. *Ego and Archetype.* New York: Viking, 1972.
Jacobi, Jolande. *Complex, Archetype, Symbol.* Princeton, NJ: Princeton Univ. Press, 1971.
Stevens, Anthony. *Archetypes: A Natural History of the Self.* New York: William Morrow, 1982.

Boy Psychology

Campbell, Joseph. *The Hero with a Thousand Faces.* Princeton, NJ: Princeton Univ. Press, 1949.

Golding, William. *The Lord of the Flies.* New York: Putnam, 1962.

Miller, Alice. *For Your Own Good: Hidden Cruelty in Child-Rearing and the Roots of Violence.* Trans. by Hildegarde and Hunter Hannum. New York: Farrar, Straus, Giroux, 1983.

Man Psychology

Bly, Robert. *Iron John: A Book About Men.* Reading, MA: Addison-Wesley, 1990.

Bolen, Jean Shinoda. *Gods in Everyman.* San Francisco: Harper & Row, 1989.

Browning, Don S. *Generative Man: Psychoanalytic Perspectives.* Philadelphia: Westminster Press, 1973.

Winnicott, D. W. *Home Is Where We Start From.* New York: Norton, 1986.

KING

Frankfort, Henri. *Kingship and the Gods.* Chicago: Univ. of Chicago Press, 1948.

Perry, John Weir. *Lord of the Four Quarters.* New York: Macmillan, 1966.

———. *Roots of Renewal in Myth and Madness: The Meaning of Psychotic Episodes.* San Francisco: Jossey-Bass, 1976.

WARRIOR

Rogers, David J. *Fighting to Win.* Garden City, NY: Doubleday, 1984.

Stevens, Anthony. *The Roots of War: A Jungian Perspective.* New York: Paragon House, 1984.

MAGICIAN

Butler, E. M. *The Myth of the Magus.* Cambridge, MA: Cambridge Univ. Press, 1948.

Neihardt, John. *Black Elk Speaks.* Lincoln: Univ. of Nebraska Press, 1968.

Nicolson, Shirley, ed. *Shamanism.* Wheaton, IL: The Theosophical Publishing House, 1987.

LOVER

Neumann, Erich. *Art and the Creative Unconscious.* Princeton, NJ: Princeton Univ. Press, 1959.

Spink, Walter M. *The Axis of Eros.* New York: Schocken Books, 1973.